*NINETEENTH CENTURY*
ESSAYS

HUMPHREY MILFORD

# ESSAYS

*MAINLY ON*

*THE NINETEENTH CENTURY*

PRESENTED TO

SIR HUMPHREY MILFORD

*Essay Index Reprint Series*

Originally published by Oxford University Press

**BOOKS FOR LIBRARIES PRESS**
FREEPORT, NEW YORK

Copyright 1948 by Oxford University Press, Inc.

Reprinted 1970 by arrangement

Reprinted from a copy in the collections of the
Brooklyn Public Library

STANDARD BOOK NUMBER:
8369-1463-5

LIBRARY OF CONGRESS CATALOG CARD NUMBER:
70-106408

PRINTED IN THE UNITED STATES OF AMERICA

# INTRODUCTION

THIS volume has been produced in honour of Humphrey Milford who, after a long and distinguished career, retired from the position of Publisher to the University of Oxford in 1945. All the contributors are personal friends, the production has been in the hands of his former colleagues at Amen House, and the book has been printed and bound in Oxford at the University Press.

Though he always said he could read anything—and to hear that he had 'stuck' in a book bearing his imprint was rare but serious news for the sponsor—beyond doubt the Victorians were his first and lasting love. It was therefore decided that, in the main, the essays in this volume should deal with Victorian topics and in particular with Victorian writers. Here are Browning, Clough, and Trollope, three whom he would place high if not highest in his affections: Browning he knows almost by heart. One of his first undertakings in retirement was to prepare a Browning selection for the World's Classics; and, earlier, he edited Clough's poems for the Oxford Miscellany. What, in less restrained company, would be described as a 'romance of publishing'—the remarkable story of Robert Bridges's popular success with *The Testament of Beauty*—is commemorated here; while the essay which throws some further sidelights on Trollope will call to mind Humphrey Milford's notable service in the recovery of Anthony Trollope from the threat of oblivion.

Not only was publishing Humphrey Milford's profession, it was surely his predestined profession, and it is therefore fitting that two of his fellows in that field should have contributed to this book: one on what publishing may often be, a hard and anxious task; the other on what we all wish it might be. No general conclusion must be drawn, however, from the fact that in the one instance the difficult author was a real person, while in the other the charming and accommodating—indeed, the ideal—author originates in dreamland!

The large and thriving Oxford music list (never forgetting the Hymnals) was a product of Humphrey Milford's courage and instinct for what was needed and could be done; and nothing could be more happily appropriate than the contribution from one who figures so largely in that list and who has been a source of encouragement from its earliest days.

This offering would not be well rounded without something on sport. Lawn tennis and cricket were the outstanding games of the versatile sportsman to whom it is presented. His eye for a ball was as true as his eye for a misprint. That he will find none in his book is more than any who know him can hope; but if he should discover none none will be discoverable.

So, this volume goes to Humphrey Milford from his friends with warm wishes for a long tale of happy years in his new Oxfordshire home.

G. F. J. C.

*November* 1947

# CONTENTS

INTRODUCTION. By G. F. J. CUMBERLEGE . . . v

I. THE RUINED COTTAGE AND THE EXCURSION. By HELEN DARBISHIRE . . . . . . . 1

II. BROWNING: A CONVERSATION. By FREDERICK PAGE . 14

III. 'SAY NOT THE STRUGGLE NOUGHT AVAILETH.' By A. L. P. NORRINGTON . . . . . . 29

IV. THE POETRY OF R. L. STEVENSON. By H. W. GARROD . 42

V. A POET IN WALTON STREET. By SIMON NOWELL-SMITH . 58

VI. PERSONAL NAMES IN TROLLOPE'S POLITICAL NOVELS. By R. W. CHAPMAN . . . . . . 72

VII. THE DIFFUSION OF IDEAS. By R. C. K. ENSOR . . 82

VIII. THE CHURCH IN THE NINETEENTH CENTURY. By R. H. MALDEN . . . . . . . 97

IX. A MINIM'S REST. By R. VAUGHAN WILLIAMS . . . 113

X. SPORTING WRITERS OF THE NINETEENTH CENTURY. By BERNARD DARWIN . . . . . . 117

XI. THE CAMEL'S BACK or the Last Tribulation of a Victorian Publisher. By MICHAEL SADLEIR . . . . . . 127

XII. THE PERFECT AUTHOR. By S. C. ROBERTS . . . 150

I

## 'THE RUINED COTTAGE' AND 'THE EXCURSION'

### A Study from the Manuscripts

#### By HELEN DARBISHIRE

WHAT we now read as the first book of *The Excursion* was originally an independent narrative poem, a stark sad tale of humble life. The transformations which the poem underwent can be traced through several manuscripts now at Dove Cottage, three fortunately complete, the earliest, alas! fragmentary.

*The Ruined Cottage*, as the original poem was known in the family circle, was greatly admired by Wordsworth's friends. Lamb recalled it with delight when he opened the newly published *Excursion* in 1814. 'My having known the story of Margaret (at the beginning),' he writes on 14 August 1814, 'a very old acquaintance even as long ago as when I first saw you at Stowey, did not make her re-appearance less fresh.' The meeting at Stowey was in July 1797. Dorothy Wordsworth, reporting, to Mary Hutchinson, Coleridge's arrival at Racedown, writes in June 1797: 'The first thing that was read after he came was Wm.'s new poem *The Ruined Cottage* with which he was much delighted.' But the poem was in existence earlier still. Wordsworth himself told Miss Fenwick (*see* I.F., Note on *The Excursion*) that the lines first written were those beginning 'Nine tedious years' and ending 'Last human tenant of these ruined walls' (Book i. 871–916): 'These were composed in 1795 at Racedown; and for several passages describing the employment and demeanour of Margaret during her affliction, I was indebted to observations made in Dorsetshire, and afterwards at Alfoxden in Somersetshire, where I resided in 1797 and 1798.' Dorothy Wordsworth wrote of it in June 1797 as Wordsworth's 'new poem', but he must have composed parts of it earlier and his own date, 1795, is probably right. The earliest version of fragments of the poem, MS. A (corresponding to portions of *Exc.* i. 502–91), is written in Wordsworth's hand on a folio sheet with watermark 1795 and includes lines which also form part of the gloomy description of the deserted cottage in *Incipient Madness*, a tentative poem, never published by Wordsworth, which is ascribed to 1795.[1] There is no complete manuscript of *The Ruined Cottage* earlier than 1798, but Coleridge quotes the last lines of Margaret's story ending 'Last human tenant of these ruined walls' in a letter to J. P. Estlin from Racedown in June 1797:

This is a lovely country and Wordsworth is a great man. . . . The lines overleaf, which I have procured Miss Wordsworth to transcribe, will I think please you.

>                                               her eye
> Was busy in the distance, shaping things
> That made her heart beat quick. Seest thou that path?
> (The greensward now has broken its grey line)
> There to and fro she paced, through many a day
> Of the warm summer: from a belt of flax
> That girt her waist, spinning the long-drawn thread
> With backward steps. Yet, ever as she passed
> A man, whose garments showed the Soldier's red,
> Or crippled mendicant in Sailor's garb,
> The little child who sat to turn the wheel,
> Ceased from his toil; and she with faltering voice,
> Expecting still to learn her husband's fate,
> Made many a fond inquiry; and when they
> Whose presence gave no comfort, were gone by,
> Her heart was still more sad.—And by yon gate
> That bars the traveller's road, she often sat,
> And if a stranger-horseman came, the latch
> Would lift, and in his face look wistfully,
> Most happy, if from aught discovered there
> Of tender feeling, she might dare repeat
> The same sad question.—Meanwhile her poor hut
> Sank to decay: for he was gone, whose hand,
> At the first nippings of October frost,
> Closed up each chink, and with fresh bands of straw
> Chequered the green-grown thatch; and so she sat
> Through the long winter, reckless and alone,
> Till this reft house by frost and thaw and rain
> Was sapped; and, when she slept, the nightly damps
> Did chill her breast, and in the stormy day

---

[1] See *Wordsworth's Poetical Works*, ed. E. de Selincourt, vol. i, p. 314.

> Her tattered clothes were ruffled by the wind,
> Even by the side of her own fire; yet still
> She loved this wretched spot nor would for worlds
> Have parted hence: and still that length of road,
> And this rude bench, one torturing hope endeared,
> Fast rooted at her heart; and, Stranger, here
> In sickness she remained, and here she died,
> —Last human tenant of these ruined walls.

This version has one telling variant from the text that we know: the narrator addresses his interlocutor as 'Stranger', not 'my friend' as in the printed text. We can tell from this that the Pedlar has been met in a casual encounter and has no intimate relation with the poet.

When in the following March Mary Hutchinson asked for a copy of *The Ruined Cottage* Dorothy Wordsworth told her of a fresh development concerning the Pedlar in the poem:

> You desire me, my dear Mary, to send you a copy of *The Ruined Cottage*. This is impossible, for it has grown to the length of 900 lines. I will however send you a copy of that part which is immediately and solely connected with the Cottage. The Pedlar's character now makes a very, certainly the most considerable part of the poem.

A complete manuscript survives, MS. B, of the version from which Dorothy quotes in this letter, and in it the poem has clearly undergone a signal change. The earlier *Ruined Cottage* known to Coleridge and Lamb in 1797, of which only fragments have survived, must have told a tale of unrelieved distress, and its setting must, I conjecture, have been as follows: the Poet on his rambles comes across a deserted Cottage which haunts his imagination (the ruined cottage in *Incipient Madness* is confirmation of this): on one of his visits to the ruin he chances to meet a Pedlar on the road, who knows, and narrates to him, the story of its 'last human tenant'. But by the spring of 1798 Wordsworth has seen his subject in a different light. The gloom has lifted. A note-book which Wordsworth used at Alfoxden between 20 January and 5 March shows him jotting down suggestions for the character of the wise and enlightened Pedlar, and in MS. B the poem opens, like Book i of *The Excursion*, with an account of the planned meeting of the Poet and his old friend, the philosophical Pedlar, whose character and background is then described at length. The wise Pedlar now takes charge of the story of Margaret and it is in the light of his faith that we are to read it.

The poem concludes with the passage quoted by Coleridge in 1797, and *The End* is written after the line
> Last human tenant of these ruined walls.

But it is significant that Wordsworth had begun to scrawl on the next pages several attempts at a reconciling passage to round off the poem. The first runs thus:

> The old man ceased: he saw that I was moved.
> From that low bench rising instinctively
> I turned away in weakness, and my heart
> Went back into the tale which he had told,
> And when at last returning from my mind
> I looked around, the cottage and the elms,
> The road, the pathway and the garden wall
> Which old and loose and mossy o'er the road
> Hung bellying, all appeared, I know not how,
> But to some eye within me all appeared
> Colours and forms of a strange discipline.
> The trouble which they sent into my thought
> Was sweet, I looked and looked again, and to myself
> I seemed a better and a wiser man.

The third holds an image of singular beauty:

> How sweetly breathes the air—it breathes most sweet
> And my heart feels it, how divinely fair
> Are yon huge clouds, how lovely are those elms
> That shew themselves with all their verdant leaves
> And all the myriad veins of those green leaves
> A luminous prospect fashioned by the sun—

But none of these beginnings proved fruitful, and he returned to another suggestion which he had inserted as an afterthought to an earlier passage of the poem, afterwards struck out,—a poignant, perhaps somewhat overwrought, description, this, of the deserted dwelling and garden:

>                               She is dead,
> The worm is on her cheek, and this poor hut
> Stripped of its outward garb of household flowers
> Of rose and sweetbriar offers to the wind
> A cold bare wall whose earthy top is tricked
> With weeds and the rank spear-grass; she is dead,

> And nettles rot and adders sun themselves
> Where we have sat together, while she nursed
> Her infant at her bosom. The wild colt,
> The unstalled heifer and the Potter's ass
> Find shelter now within the chimney walls
> Where I have seen her evening hearth-stone blaze
> And through the window spread upon the road
> Its cheerful light. You will forgive me, Sir,
> I feel I play the truant with my tale.

On second thoughts, writing on the verso of the preceding page, he substituted for the last line and a half the following:

> But I have spoken thus
> With an ungrateful temper and have read
> The forms of things with an unworthy eye.
> She sleeps in the calm earth and peace is here.
> I well remember that those very plumes,
> Those weeds and the high spear-grass on that wall,
> By mist and silent rain-drops silvered o'er
> As once I passed, did to my heart convey
> So still an image of tranquillity,
> So calm and still, and looked so beautiful,
> Amid the uneasy thoughts which filled my mind
> That what we feel of sorrow and despair
> From ruin and from change, and all the grief
> The passing shows of being leave behind
> Appeared an idle dream that could not live
> Where meditation was.[1] I turned away
> And walked along my path in happiness.
> You will forgive me, Sir, I feel I play
> The truant with my tale. Poor Margaret—

It was this beautiful afterthought but with a different opening,

> Be wise and chearful; and no longer read
> The forms of things with an unworthy eye.

that he was to use in the end to lift his unhappy tale at its conclusion to the level of faith and hope on which his mind moved in 1798.

[1] The preceding lines were printed thus in the first edition of *The Excursion*, 1814. The later editions, from 1845 onwards, give a definitely Christian turn to the thought, which does not belong to Wordsworth's early conception of the Pedlar.

These unforgettable lines of reconciliation, haunting and moving as they are, have always held me up with one slight check. What were the *forms of things* which the poet is rebuked for reading with an unworthy eye? The answer is given in the abandoned passage I have quoted. In a mood of anguished sympathy the onlooker has read the rank spear-grass and the weeds as emblems of desolation and ruin: in another mood, one of serene meditation, he sees in them an image of tranquillity and beauty.

The sacrifice of the heightened passage about the deserted house and garden is responsible for another missing link. The line

> Last *human* tenant of these ruined walls

loses the lively body of its implied reference when the cottage loses its non-human tenants, the wild colt, the unstalled heifer, and the Potter's ass.

In the addendum to MS. B the beautiful lines of reconciliation, with the image of the spear-grass, just quoted, come as the culmination of a long reflective harangue from the Pedlar (most of which was afterwards incorporated in the fourth book of *The Excursion*) on the beneficent effect on man of a sympathy with nature; it opens thus:

> Not useless do I deem
> These quiet sympathies with things that hold
> An inarticulate language; for the man
> Once taught to love such objects as excite
> No morbid passions, no disquietude,
> No vengeance and no hatred needs must feel
> The joy of that pure principle of love
> So deeply that unsatisfied with aught
> Less pure and exquisite he cannot choose
> But seek for objects of a kindred love
> In fellow-natures and a kindred joy.
> Accordingly he by degrees perceives
> His feelings of aversion softened down,
> A holy tenderness pervades his frame,
> His sanity of reason not impaired,
> Say rather all his thoughts now flowing clear,
> From a clear fountain flowing, he looks round,
> He seeks for good and finds the good he seeks.

Coleridge quotes these opening lines in a letter to his brother George in April 1798 to clinch his statement of his own faith:

I love fields and woods and mountains with almost a visionary fondness. And because I have found benevolence and quietness growing within me as that fondness has increased therefore I should wish to be the means of implanting it in others, and to destroy bad passions not by combating them but by keeping them in inaction.

The close of this harangue of the Pedlar is told in simpler and more pregnant words than those of the corresponding passage in *The Excursion* (iv. 1275–97). We can measure the distance the Poet was to travel between 1798 and 1814 by placing the two passages side by side.

> The old man ceased.
> The words he uttered shall not pass away,
> They had sunk into me, but not as sounds
> To be expressed by visible characters,
> For while he spake my spirit had obeyed
> The presence of his eye, my ear had drunk
> The meaning of his voice. He had discoursed
> Like one who in the slow and silent works,
> The manifold conclusions of his thought,
> Had brooded till Imagination's power
> Condensed them to a passion whence she drew
> Herself new energies, resistless force.
>                                       MS. 1798.

> Here closed the Sage that eloquent harangue,
> Poured forth with fervour in continuous stream;
> Such as, remote, 'mid savage wilderness,
> An Indian Chief discharges from his breast
> Into the hearing of the assembled Tribes,
> In open circle seated round, and hushed
> As the unbreathing air, when not a leaf
> Stirs in the mighty woods.—So did he speak:
> The words he uttered shall not pass away;
> For they sank into me—the bounteous gift
> Of One whom time and nature had made wise,
> Gracing his language with authority
> Which hostile spirits silently allow;

> Of One in whom persuasion and belief
> Had ripened into faith, and faith become
> A passionate intuition; whence the Soul,
> Though bound to Earth by ties of pity and love,
> From all injurious servitude was free.
>
> *The Excursion*, 1814.

In the earlier passage the experience seems something we can touch and feel at first-hand; in the later, thought and art have put it through a refining process. There is more loss than gain.

The next complete manuscript of the poem, MS. D, must have been written soon after MS. B. In it Wordsworth tries the experiment of cutting away the bulky accretion of the Pedlar's background, about 260 lines of MS. B. This leaves a compact poem, rightly entitled *The Ruined Cottage*, divided into two parts, the first of 197 lines, the second of 320. The division comes at the line

> The calm of nature with our restless thoughts.
>
> *Exc.* i. 604.

This manuscript does not give us back the crude original *Ruined Cottage*, for the philosophical Pedlar, friend of the Poet's boyhood, introduces and guides the narrative. But it gives us the ripe and well-proportioned poem that grew out of that crude original; Margaret's story is the main theme and stands out in its sheer naked beauty. In the opening lines the Pedlar is met, and is allowed, with no further preliminary than the heated Poet's slaking his thirst at the Cottage well, to begin his reminiscences of Margaret. Wordsworth must at this time have felt a misgiving about the double-barrelled form which the poem had taken: his growing interest in the Pedlar's character had been leading him to combine two subjects in one poem. Perhaps, he now reflects, they had better be separated. The abandoned lines on the Pedlar are accordingly copied in as addenda with the idea of using them in some other connexion.

But the Pedlar was not so easily to be disengaged from the story of Margaret, and when in the winter of 1801–2 Wordsworth again became preoccupied with the poem he reintroduced the Pedlar with different antecedents and a background

'THE EXCURSION' 9

still further elaborated. In MS. B he had been called Armytage, and had been born and brought up as a shepherd on the Cumbrian hills: now he is Patrick Drummond, a Scotsman, who as a boy tended cattle in Perthshire, and later made his Pedlar's headquarters at Hawkshead:

> We were dear Friends; I from my childhood up
> Had known him, in a nook of Furness Fells
> At Hawkshead, where I went to school nine years.
> One room he had, a fifth part of a house,
> A place to which he drew from time to time
> And found a kind of home or harbour there.

Dorothy Wordsworth's Journals reveal that between December 1801 and March 1802 Wordsworth subjected the poem to much anxious consideration and a protracted revision. In all but one of the twenty references the poem is now, significantly, called *The Pedlar*. Here are some of the entries:

1801 DEC. 21. Wm. sate beside me, and read *The Pedlar*. He was in good spirits, and full of hope of what he should do with it.
DEC. 22. Wm. composed a few lines of *The Pedlar*.
DEC. 27. Mary wrote some lines of the third part of Wm.'s poem, which he brought to read to us.
1802 JAN. 26. Wm. wrote out part of his poem and endeavoured to alter it, and so made himself ill.
JAN. 30. Wm. worked at *The Pedlar* all morning. He kept the dinner waiting till 4 o'clock. He was much tired.
FEB. 7. We sate by the fire and . . . read *The Pedlar*, thinking it done; but lo! though Wm. could find fault with no one part of it, it was uninteresting, and must be altered. Poor Wm.!
FEB. 10. We read the first part of the poem and were delighted with it, but Wm. afterwards got to some ugly place, and went to bed tired out.
MARCH 3. I was so unlucky as to propose to rewrite *The Pedlar*. Wm. got to work, and was worn to death.
MARCH 6. I wrote *The Pedlar* and finished it.
MARCH 7. I stitched up *The Pedlar*.

An addendum to MS. D clearly records a part of this revision and the main results of it are copied out in the next manuscript, MS. E, which divides the poem into three parts at l. 433 and l. 604, divisions which he continued to mark in the latest editions of *The Excursion*. The first division is devoted wholly to the Pedlar. Here, as in MS. B, the poem has two centres of interest, the Pedlar, and the Ruined Cottage with its last human inmate, and the Pedlar has pride of place. Wordsworth now regarded the poem as finished and was considering plans for publication. On 10 March 1802 Dorothy writes: 'Wm. has since tea been talking of publishing the Yorkshire Wolds poem [i.e. *Hartleap Well*] with *The Pedlar*.' But no step was taken. A further manuscript version, MS. M, closely following MS. E, was copied by Dorothy in March 1804 in the companion volume to that which she was preparing for Coleridge to take with him on his voyage to Malta.

At what date precisely he ceased to regard *The Pedlar* as a separate poem and began to plan *The Excursion* as a development of it is not revealed, but it is evident that he came to find in the character of the Pedlar, later to be called the Wanderer, an effective starting-point for this section of his projected philosophical poem, and by the end of 1804 he is writing of *The Pedlar* as a part of *The Recluse*.

25 DEC. 1804. [Wordsworth to Sir George Beaumont.]
I do not know if you are exactly acquainted with the plan of my poetical labour: it is twofold; first a Poem to be called *The Recluse*; in which it will be my object to express in verse my most interesting feelings concerning Man, Nature, and Society; and next, a Poem on my earlier life or the growth of my own mind. . . . This latter work I expect to have finished before the month of May; and then I purpose to fall with all my might upon the former which is the chief object upon which my thoughts have been fixed these many years. Of this poem, that of *The Pedlar*, which Coleridge read you, is part, and I may have written of it altogether about 2,000 lines. It will consist, I hope, of almost 10 or 12 thousand.

*The Excursion* was published in 1814 under the title *The Excursion: a portion of the Recluse*, and the Preface affirms his original purpose, the

determination to compose a philosophical Poem, containing views of Man, Nature and Society; and to be entitled *The Recluse*; as having for its principal subject the sensations or opinions of a Poet living in retirement. . . . The first and third parts of *The Recluse* will consist chiefly of meditations in the Author's own Person; ... in the intermediate part (*The Excursion*) the intervention of Characters speaking is employed, and something of a dramatic form adopted.

Coleridge's plan for Wordsworth's philosophical poem was that he 'should assume the station of a man in mental repose, one whose principles were made up, and so prepared to deliver upon authority a system of philosophy'. But this was what, try as he would, Wordsworth could never bring himself to do. His method of work in preparation for the great poem was, as his note-books show, to write down, with the hope of using them later, fragments of philosophical reflection, of natural observation, and also tales and character-studies from real life. When in the autumn of 1804, with Coleridge departed to Malta, he seriously set to work on a portion of *The Recluse*, it was perhaps inevitable that it should take the form, not of 'meditations in the author's own person', but of an arrangement of narratives interspersed with reflections, upon a slender dramatic basis. It is clear as day that, though *The Excursion* came to embody some of the ideas set forth by Coleridge, its poetic form did not originate in the much-pondered plan for *The Recluse* but in an independent tale, *The Ruined Cottage*, written before Wordsworth became intimate with Coleridge.

Now there were strong objections to using the story of Margaret for the opening book of *The Excursion*. Its natural scene is altogether incongruous with that of the body of the poem. The bare, scorching plain, the solitary cottage well, rank weeds, and grass-grown walls which belong properly to Margaret's Dorsetshire setting have no relation at all with the scene of the Langdales, where the main action of *The Excursion* goes forward amid bleak mountain valleys, alive with becks and waterfalls. It is useless to say that the *place* is after all of little significance. Places meant as much to Wordsworth's imagination as people: they belonged together to the vital substance of his poetry. Who shall say whether the thorntree and the little mound and pond on the wild hill-side are responsible for touching into beauty and mystery the crude suffering of the woman in *The Thorn*, or whether the human passions, rather, have mysteriously transformed the dreary place?

Certain it is that in some of his greatest poems the place and the human life that belonged to it, moulded it, and was moulded by it, are *one* subject. The Ruined Cottage is one of these significant Wordsworthian subjects: the title is of its essence. And Margaret, in the poet's eyes, owes her unforgettable appeal to the place where she lived:

> Her person and her face
> Were homely such as none who pass her by
> Would have remembered, yet when she was seen
> In her own dwelling place a grace was hers
> And Beauty, which beginning from without
> Fell back on her with sanctifying power.
>         (Unpublished fragment.)

Would Wordsworth have been wiser if he had kept *The Ruined Cottage* as an independent poem, and devised another opening for *The Excursion*? I should be sorry to rob *The Excursion* of its best book, and I freely admit that the Pedlar deserves his apotheosis as the Wanderer. But I must hold that *The Ruined Cottage* occupied a unique place in Wordsworth's poetic development: it was the first great poem in which he sounded the depths of our common nature, and it deserved to be published in its original independence and integrity.

But this is an impatient answer (and all Wordsworthians must learn patience) to what was after all a fruitless question. For the truth is that *The Excursion* would never have been written at all without the Pedlar of *The Ruined Cottage* to give it the initial impetus, and to act as its presiding genius. Without Book i we should never have had Book iv. For several years Wordsworth had been trying, with Coleridge at his elbow, to get the great philosophical poem under way, but except for the first book of *The Recluse*—really a continuation of his autobiography from the point where *The Prelude* left off—he had been able to produce nothing but fragments.

We must take Wordsworth as we find him, an inspired poet, a not always inspiring teacher, a fine but fallible artist. We must take *The Excursion* for what it is, a disconcerting great poem, a collection of superlatively good things with others not so good, arranged in a structure which for all its thoughtful planning lacks the inevitability of organic life, yet still a great poem, yielding passages of high poetry unique and irreplaceable between low-lying tracts of capable verse.

And now, with the manuscripts to guide us, we may, if we will, take *The Ruined Cottage* as a separate poem, a true work of art, possessing in a rare degree the simplicity of form and depth of meaning which Wordsworth could give to his creations in those early years, when he first saw into the life of things.

## II
## BROWNING: A CONVERSATION
### *By* FREDERICK PAGE

*Scene:* SIBYLLA'S *drawing-room, 31 December 1889*

ATTICUS *is in town for a few days.* FRANCES *and* COLIN *have dropped in to tea. Two Professors are coming on from the Funeral at the Abbey.*

SIBYLLA: We are to have Mr. Saintsbury and Mr. Ker with us this afternoon, Atticus.
ATTICUS (*resignedly*): Ah, yes?
SIBYLLA: Oh, no! You mustn't say it like that. I want you not to be chilly with them.
ATTICUS: Am I not the most amiable of old gentlemen?
SIBYLLA: Not always. And you mustn't be perverse if the talk turns on Mr. Browning, as it inevitably will. Frances and Colin, here, are Browning's devotees, and your disciples.
ATTICUS: I am glad that they discriminate.
FRANCES: We don't set you so far apart as perhaps you might expect.

*But here the Professors arrive.* SIBYLLA *pours out tea,* COLIN *hands the cups and the cakes. The ceremony at the Abbey is discussed, and the crowd is mentioned.*

SIBYLLA: Yes, "Mr. Browning's public is now great and various. One cannot ignore that it is not limited to the lovers of poetry purely."[1]
ATTICUS: I would like you to convince me that Browning has any great quantity of what is purely poetry.
SIBYLLA: True it is that "his work may undergo division, selection, and rejection, and suffer no loss".
SAINTSBURY: We should all agree with each other's inclusions, and disagree with the exclusions!
SIBYLLA: We should have to take some notice of the charge of obscurity. I think that "no author should be blamed for

[1] The words between "double quotes" are throughout those of my originals. Nothing else is historical, and anachronisms abound.

## BROWNING: A CONVERSATION

obscurity provided that he has done his best to be intelligible, nor should any pains be grudged in the effort to understand him. Difficulty of thought is the very heart of poetry."

ATTICUS: Not the logician's or the metaphysician's difficult thought! But of course you don't mean that.

SIBYLLA: No. Dante's, or Wordsworth's.

ATTICUS: Browning's argufying?

SIBYLLA: "His thought is knotted—is as knotty indeed as a fugue. But no one who has not followed him through his labours of analysis, can understand the pleasure of the more studious reader"—forgive me, Atticus; *your* studies have lain elsewhere—"one's pleasure at hearing Mr. Browning's cool, strong, argumentative voice break in the rare note of emotion, caused by his sudden rise to a higher moral and mental beauty. When this happens, not the feeling only, but the verse, softens and relaxes. When that higher fresher thought comes, it brings with it its own inevitable music."

COLIN: Its music! But Atticus has said that one "stumbles over the hillocks of potsherds and broken brickbats" of Browning's rhythm and diction.

W. P. KER: Why, certainly there is something in Browning that makes that description as plausible as it is witty.

SAINTSBURY: I think we shall not find that 'something' very easy to locate in the rhythm. "Browning, though an audacious, is almost invariably a correct prosodist—he goes often to the very verge, but hardly ever over it."

KER: Without o'erflowing, full.

SAINTSBURY: And "when he chooses (which is not so extremely seldom) he can be as smooth as smooth". I can concede just half a point to Atticus, that "not very seldom, likewise, he set his affected eccentricity of tongue against his native justness of ear. But even then the ear generally won."

COLIN: I am glad, Sir, you speak of his justness of ear, for that is what has been most borne in upon me, in my recent re-readings.

KER: But Atticus has asked how he is to disinter the soft pearl of distinction from the—well, you *did* say it, Sir—from the heaped potsherds and broken brickbats of a violent and self-imposed originality of diction.

SAINTSBURY: But Atticus might have asked himself how we could reasonably expect to find the peculiar aroma of Browning's personality in 'the imaginary utterances of imaginary persons, not his own'. Were Caliban, Sludge, Blougram, Hohenstiel-Schwangau, Count Guido—his 'fifty men and women'—his hundred or more men and women—to speak with Browning's own voice? The surprising thing is that they do, that they inevitably must; that is, their inventor inevitably must. Not even Dickens could come nearer to Sludge—Sludge in his abject self, Sludge in his vile dialect—than Browning does. And yet Sludge remains Browning, Browning remains Browning, in that it is Browning's voice, Browning's ear, that controls the line, the verse. The jargon is but overlaid on Browning's English.

SIBYLLA: But we are used to that failure in mimicry: Meredith's people speak like Meredith, Henry James's like James. It is Trollope's people who always speak (and write letters) like themselves. Hardy's rustics we take on trust. And as for mimicry, the more perfect the more trivial, surely?

COLIN: I wonder if Mr. Saintsbury's word 'control' does not give us just what we want, to reconcile Atticus to those fearful monologues. I had found the word 'volubility' for Browning, or rather for his dramatis personae, and have since found that Mr. Saintsbury and Mr. Symonds had used it already, but I think we haven't Browning's secret till we say 'controlled volubility'. 'Control' is the essential word. He seems to give Sludge and Blougram their head, and one fears they will be interminably voluble——

SAINTSBURY: Yes, you will remember Bagehot's friend who always looked ahead to see how much he had let himself in for—'what length of intellectual adventure he was about to commence'!

COLIN: ——but it is Browning who controls their argument— they think they have freedom of speech, but their creator has fore-knowledge absolute.

FRANCES: Or not quite absolute. Dear Sibylla, you have written of the 'uncontrasted ignominy' of Blougram. Browning thought he had given his Bishop a sufficient foil in the incorruptible simplicity of Gigadibs. It is unlikely that he foreknew that in a few years he would be writing "A Death in the Desert". In that poem, Atticus, each one of a little group of St. John's disciples had suffered or was to suffer martyrdom for the faith in which the Apostle was dying. Browning did not leave Blougram uncontrasted.

KER: He reappears as a Cardinal in *The Ring and the Book*, to serve as a foil to the heroic priest Caponsacchi.

COLIN: It is the argument that justifies (and inspired) those poems. Re-reading, after a long interval, "Blougram", "Sludge", and "Prince Hohenstiel-Schwangau" one wonders, as one gets nearer and nearer to the end, however Browning is going to explode their sophistries. He knew from the first.

SIBYLLA: But if we speak of volubility and control we must also speak of compression. Surely never, never, in all literature was more compressed into two lines than the anguished appeal of the wife-murderer against the sentence of the Pope:

> Abate,—Cardinal,—Christ,—Maria,—God, . . .
> Pompilia, will you let them murder me?

And, Atticus, that is Browning's conception: his creature's abject terror, his own dramatic irony, his the divine satire which is pity.

ATTICUS: "The iron muscle and electric nerve."

SAINTSBURY: But that compression is frequent in Browning. Consider the drama in this "epigram" (in the Greek sense). It is Eurydice to Orpheus:

> But give them me, the mouth, the eyes, the brow!
> Let them once more absorb me! One look now
>   Will lap me round for ever, not to pass
> Out of its light, though darkness lie beyond;
> Hold me but safe again within the bond
>   Of one immortal look! All woe that was,
> Forgotten, and all terror that may be,
> Defied,—no past is mine, no future: look at me!

SIBYLLA: A kingly gift to Leighton for his picture.

FRANCES: So now we have represented to Atticus that Browning has a right to his subjects, to his arguments, to his dramatis personae (with whatever degree of mimicry he found worth while or irresistible). It only remains for us—doesn't it?—to demonstrate the verse as—well, as *not* predominantly what Atticus said it was.

ATTICUS: Thank you, Frances. It is sweet of you to spare me those "brickbats"!

COLIN: We will never mention them again. But I should like to call up a reinforcement on your side in the unexpected person of Mr. Stevenson.
KER: R.L.S.! But he isn't anti-Browning, surely?
COLIN: No indeed! he has spoken of *The Ring and the Book* as 'a poem, one of the noblest of our century'. But listen to what he has said of *The Inn-Album*, a poem which I think fully deserves the same description. In an anonymous review,[1] of which he has confessed the authorship, he wrote:

> When Mr. Browning finds a line shambling out from underneath him in a loose mess of unaccented syllables; when he finds it, like an ill-made blanc-mange, subside into a squash or quagmire instead of standing on its own basis with a certain sort of dignity or strength—quick, says Mr. Browning, break it up into an unexpected parenthesis, choke off the reader with a dash, leave him clinging at the verse's end to a projecting conjunction, cut a somersault before him, flick off his hat with your toe in true Mabille fashion; in short, do what you will so you bewilder him, and the limping verse will get away to cover undetected.

ATTICUS: Well, that's pretty spirited!
COLIN: Oh, yes! I can safely offer you Mr. Stevenson's support, for never were accusations more preposterous, more wanton. Precisely and especially what the verse of *The Inn-Album* does is never to shamble, never to limp. No verse ever trod more firmly, none was ever more tightly packed—packed tight with the story. Never was story-telling more controlled. No single thing is said that is not meant to *tell* again, later. Mr. Stevenson says that it took him five minutes (him! the most parsimonious of story-tellers in prose) to realize that the woman had, at the end of the poem, committed suicide. It should not have done: the verse had told him that, nine times (as I counted). It took *me* five minutes to realize that the younger man would not be charged with the murder of the elder man. It should not have done. Mr. Symonds and another writer[2] say that we cannot give the woman our respect. We must. The story answers all the questions we can put to it; and always, always, Browning controls the verse.

[1] In *Vanity Fair*, 11 Dec. 1875, partly reprinted in *Notes and Queries*, 12 Feb. 1944.
[2] In, respectively, the *Academy*, 27 Nov. 1875, and *Notes and Queries*, 25 March 1876.

FRANCES: Yes, the verse. If we can convert Atticus to that, he will find all the poetry we have found, and more too. Mr. Ker, do start us off!

KER: Let us concede to Atticus that a great deal of Browning *looks* like

> Peter Piper picked a peck of pickled pepper

but "it is wrong to take the harsh colliding consonants as a true sample of Browning's art". They are there on the printed page, and only there. They are not in the verse as a lover of verse would speak it.

SAINTSBURY: Yes, Browning as much as any poet teaches us how he would have his verses read; and, so read, they *are* verses; it *is* verse, the verse of a master. His 'harshnesses' prove to be none at all when our voice follows his, note by note, as with sympathy and goodwill it learns to do.

ATTICUS: You remind me of Father Hopkins. You don't know his verse yet, but Mr. Bridges means to print it some day: I can't think what people will make of it! When I had to tell Mr. Hopkins how little I could like his—his—well, in brief, *his* "brickbats" he wrote to me,[1] "But take breath and read it with the ears, as I always wish to be read, and my verse becomes all right." And you would say this on behalf of Browning?

FRANCES: I want to say for him no less than that he was a veritable connoisseur of verbal loveliness—of which, four examples crowd upon me at once. His Aristophanes is trying to recall a girl's name: he remembers that it was

> some rich name,
> Vowel-buds thorned about with consonants,
> Fragrant, felicitous, rose-glow enriched
> By the Isle's unguent,

and after making many shots at it, he recaptures the name itself: Balaustion. Then there's another name, that of a Paris jeweller who has given a notable diamond to bedeck the image of Our Lady:

> the liquid name
> 'Miranda',—faceted as lovelily
> As his own gift.

---

[1] Actually to Bridges.

And then a flower's name:

>This flower she stopped at, finger on lip,
>  Stooped over, in doubt, as settling its claim;
>Till she gave me, with pride to make no slip,
>  Its soft meandering Spanish name:
>What a name! Was it love or praise?
>  Speech half-asleep or song half-awake?
>I must learn Spanish, one of these days,
>  Only for that slow sweet name's sake.

ATTICUS: I could wish, Frances, that those were my verses, and you reading them. Tell me some more.

FRANCES: Well, a phrase this time: Miss Thackeray's, in Browning's appreciation of it: 'call the land' (it is Normandy)—

> call the land
>By one slow hither-thither stretching, fast
>Subsiding-into-slumber sort of name,
>Symbolic of the place and people too,
>White Cotton Night-cap Country. Excellent!

COLIN:

>He who blows through bronze can breathe through silver,

and often enough he does.

SIBYLLA: Mr. Saintsbury says that our voice must follow Browning's, note by note. I think we can hear in Browning's verse that his was 'a scrupulous precision of enunciation'.[1] His 'usual' is always three syllables; his 'real', of course, has a diphthong, we can hear it. His 'naturally' is always four rippling, undulating syllables; his 'squirrel' always two equal syllables. His polysyllables always ripple, necessarily when one of them fills the second half of an alexandrine:

> he will buy
>Up the whole stock of earth's uncharitableness,

but also habitually:

> soul
>As supernaturally grand, as face
>Was fair beyond example.
> sent a-slide
>My folly, falteringly, stumblingly,
>Down, down, and deeper down.

[1] Cyril Bailey on J. W. Mackail.

# BROWNING: A CONVERSATION

KER: I would instance one line as putting Browning along with Tennyson as a prosodist,

> All in quantity, careful of his motion,
> Like the skater on ice that hardly bears him.

ATTICUS: And that line is——?
KER: Just this:

> There flashed the propriety, expediency . . .

ATTICUS: Very thin ice! But I agree that it does bear you.
KER: Well, here's another like it:

> Guido, clandestinely, irrevocably . . .

SIBYLLA: But I should have said that Browning, in general, seems "intentionally to ignore quantity".
COLIN: Do you mean that ten-syllable lines of his often have more than five accents?
SIBYLLA: I am willing that you should put it that way.
COLIN: But the line isn't clogged or huddled. The syllables and the accents make room for each other, *mingling like flood with equal flood In agitated ease.* (ATTICUS *shows himself pleased with this application of his own verse.*) COLIN (*continues*): But I confess I could not always mark the accents with confidence.
ATTICUS: What need, if the lines *do* convince the ear? Try a few of them on us.
COLIN: These are all from the *Inn-Album*, so that I am putting Mr. Stevenson in the dock:

> The lady's proud pale queenliness of scorn.
> Should life prove half true life's term, death the rest.
>                                     Lay these words
> To heart then, or where God meant heart should lurk.
> Yes! leave this youth, as he leaves you, as I
> Leave each.
> In folly beyond field-flower-foolishness.
> Some parson, some smug crop-haired smooth-skinned sort
> Of curate-creature.
> Sun-warmth, dew-coolness,—squirrel, bee and bird.

ATTICUS: I don't like turning Queen's evidence against my fellow prisoner, but *I* should pass those lines.

COLIN: There is one habit which rules Browning's verse, measures it, makes it verse. It isn't a mannerism, for it is everywhere in literature, but it is so laughably (when one has become conscious of it) ubiquitous in Browning, that it must be his method: a method of accumulation—a string of adjectives attached to one noun, one nominative with three or more predicates, one predicate to three or more nominatives, or a succession of phrases of one pattern, set in apposition. He has most of this in common with every writer, with Henry James, for example, in whose prose,[1] also, it sometimes, naughtily, makes verse:

> unhurried, unflurried, unworried
> sifting, selecting, comparing

or—and this might be Clough—

> dazed a little, no doubt, breathless, no doubt, and bewildered.

But now see how it works in Browning:

> Murder's proved
> With five—what we call qualities of bad,
> Worse, worst, and yet worse still, and still worse yet.

ATTICUS: Poor Lindley Murray with his bare three degrees of comparison!

COLIN: Oh, Browning can do it again:

> Rare, rarer, rarest, not rare but unique.

These next lines are notorious, and I know that some Catholics take them in bad part, but I think we must allow Browning the good humour of his ill humour. He hadn't found the librarians at the Vatican sympathetic or helpful with his researches, and the less so that he was a Protestant:

> 'Go, get you manned by Manning and new-manned
> By Newman and, mayhap, wise-manned to boot
> By Wiseman, and we'll see or else we won't!'

And now for eight adjectives, six of them hyphenated, to one noun:

> A husband, poor, care-bitten, sorrow-sunk,
> Little, long-nosed, bush-bearded, lantern-jawed,
> Forty-six-years full.

[1] In *The Ambassadors*, not then written!

ATTICUS: Yes, that *makes* the verse, as you say, and as it would not in Urquhart's Rabelais.
COLIN: But you must let the "method" make verse in this line although Browning printed it without commas and without my pauses:

> a priest,
> Smooth-mannered,   soft-speeched,   sleek-cheeked visitor.

ATTICUS: As Mr. Saintsbury said, the reader must bring a great deal of goodwill to such a line. But you read it very well.
COLIN: Thank you, Atticus. But this line reads itself:

> The lout-lord, bully-beggar, braggart-sneak.

ATTICUS: If Urquhart weren't unsurpassable, Browning might have given us a new version.
SAINTSBURY: Since you say that, you must certainly read his *Aristophanes' Apology*.
FRANCES: It is for something the farthest in the world from Rabelais that I want to offer Atticus something from *Aristophanes' Apology*.
ATTICUS: Good! Come on, Frances. Colin has had the argument in his hands long enough!
FRANCES: I suppose one might almost define Browning as a poet who never donned a singing-robe.
COLIN (*quoting* ATTICUS *again*): *To strut on stilts was not his use.*
FRANCES: But if he never wrote in the Grand Manner, he was capable of the great style.—Atticus, I am going to show you yourself in Browning.
ATTICUS: I say!
FRANCES: Yes, I am! Balaustion and her husband, after the fall of Athens and the death of their adored Euripides, have taken ship for Rhodes. Now you are to think that Athens was for them what England is to you—to us. You are to recall your own dark forebodings of our future, your stern joy in the well-deserved disaster you foresee for us, your serene certitude in a world once more sane after our empire has perished like all the empires before us:

> *A dim heroic Nation, long since dead,*
> *The foulness of her agony forgot.*

ATTICUS: Frances, you bring the tears to my eyes.

FRANCES: No, you are to think of literature only, just now. Is not this in the great style?—

> What else in life seems piteous any more
> After such pity, or proves terrible
> Besides such terror?

And would not you be glad—would not Landor have been proud—to sign these lines?—

> Why should despair be? Since, distinct above
> Man's wickedness and folly, flies the wind
> And floats the cloud, free transport for one soul
> Out of its fleshly durance dim and low,—
> Since disembodied soul anticipates
> (Thought-borne as now, in rapturous unrestraint)
> Above all crowding, crystal silentness,
> Above all noise, a silver solitude:—
> . . . . . . . .
> O nothing doubt, Philemon! Greed and strife,
> Hatred and cark and care, what place have they
> In yon blue liberality of heaven?
> How the sea helps! How rose-smit earth will rise
> Breast-high thence, some bright morning, and be Rhodes!
> Heaven, earth and sea, my warrant—in their name,
> Believe—o'er falsehood, truth is surely sphered,
> O'er ugliness beams beauty, o'er this world
> Extends that realm where, 'as the wise assert',
> Philemon, thou shalt see Euripides
> Clearer than mortal sense perceived the man!

SIBYLLA: Thank you, Frances.
ATTICUS: Yes, indeed. But, Sibylla, what was it you had in your mind when you spoke of Browning's argumentative voice breaking in emotion, and softening into music?
SIBYLLA: This, from his early drama, *The Return of the Druses*. "There is some difficulty in the character of Anael with her double love and her half-deliberate delusion, so that much of the verse allotted to her is intricate enough; but where strong single feeling rises in the heart of this exiled Druse girl, what exquisite music sweeps out indeliberately!—

> Dost thou snow-swathe thee kinglier, Lebanon,
> Than in my dreams?"

ATTICUS: Exquisite, as you say.
KER: Yes. One used to read Browning for his doctrine, for his fun, for the pride in having read him. Now one reads him for his verse, for its *not* infrequent beauty, because, indeed, "what Browning has to give us is not knowledge only, nor strength, but beauty. The simplest and most satisfactory name for it is poetry."
SIBYLLA: And nothing is more English than magic in poetry. Not even Mr. Arnold could call Browning Celtic.
ATTICUS: He has no 'horns of Elfland faintly blowing'?
SAINTSBURY: Not Elfland, and not faintly, but "Childe Roland to the Dark Tower came".
ATTICUS: Yes, I cannot pretend to be ignorant of that wonderful poem. And I won't ask you to match Keats's

> magic casements opening on the foam
> Of perilous seas in faery lands forlorn.

KER: What of this?—

>                       the sprinkled isles,
> Lily on lily, that o'erlace the sea,
> And laugh their pride when the light wave lisps
>     'Greece'—

ATTICUS: Lovely! you embolden me to ask for something comparable with

> A damsel with a dulcimer
> In a vision once I saw

and the rest of it.
COLIN: "Women and Roses" begins promisingly:

> I dream of a red-rose tree.
> And which of its roses three
> Is the dearest rose to me?
>
> Round and round, like a dance of snow
> In a dazzling drift, as its guardians, go
> Floating the women faded for ages,
> Sculptured in stone on the poet's pages.
> Then follow women fresh and gay,
> Living and loving and loved to-day.
> Last, in the rear, flee the multitude of maidens,
> Beauties yet unborn. And all to one cadence,
> They circle their rose on my rose tree.

But then the poem becomes a riddle that defeats me.

ATTICUS: "One of those things that, as Lord Dundreary said, no fellow can be expected to understand?"
SAINTSBURY: Well, W. P., there's a great deal more that we should like to discuss, or to quote, but I think that you and I should be getting off to the Athenaeum now.
ATTICUS: But will you not, each of you, before you go, to complete my subjugation, read me one perfect thing? Mr. Saintsbury?
SAINTSBURY: I think this should fetch you, for it might be your own Sussex marshes:

> Where the quiet-coloured end of evening smiles,
>     Miles and miles
> On the solitary pastures where our sheep
>     Half-asleep
> Tinkle homeward thro' the twilight, stray or stop
>     As they crop—
> Was the site of a city great and gay,
>     (So they say)

but I need not go on.
ATTICUS: Yes, that could be Romney Marsh. And Mr. Ker?
KER: We all read so much, and so quickly, and forget so soon, and perhaps the metre of "Waring" has rushed us so, that we do not remember how "the verse changes from its loose variety into the sounding 'square' verse—the old heroic measure"—how it changes into this, at the thought of Iphigenia:

> To Dian's fane at Taurica,
> Where now a captive priestess, she alway
> Mingles her tender grave Hellenic speech
> With theirs, tuned to the hailstone-beaten beach:
> As pours some pigeon, from the myrrhy lands
> Rapt by the whirlblast to fierce Scythian strands
> Where breed the swallows, her melodious cry
> Amid their barbarous twitter.

[*And with this, and with New Year wishes, the two professors take their leave.*]

ATTICUS: And so, Colin, Browning has no difficulties for you?
COLIN: O, but he has! Occasionally he has a phrase which one thinks of as one and indivisible, and he divides it between two lines, and then I cannot tell how to speak those two lines as two verses.

ATTICUS: Yes, that is serious, isn't it! But let us have some examples.
COLIN: Here are three:

> So, Pope I meant to make myself, by step
> And step, whereof the first should be to find
> A perfect woman.
>                     I was not my own,
> No longer had the eyes to see, the ears
> To hear, the mind to judge, since heart and soul
> Now were another's.
>                     In some Salaminian cave
> Where sky and sea and solitude make earth
> And man and noise one insignificance.

ATTICUS: They crave wary walking. But now you two young people must do as your elders have done, and each give me one more thing of beauty to be a joy for ever. Frances, you shall have the woman's last word.
COLIN (*whose turn comes first*): Well, Sir, I have heard of a man who could always enhearten himself with this great mouth-filling, heart-stirring fragment:

> Bring forth all my war![1]

But for me, I have two lines of Browning, and they happen to come from one of the very few passages where he speaks in his own person. In Normandy he had become interested in an awful story of real local life. Some poor young fool was drifting towards self-destruction, and Browning thinks: "If only he could have been directed to my friend Milsand who lives only a few miles away!" and then through a page or more he pays his tribute to his friend's probity, his sagacity, his helpfulness: "What hinders that my heart relieve itself?" and then come my two lines:

> O friend, who makest warm my wintry world,
> And wise my heaven, if there we consort too.

SIBYLLA: O beautiful masculine friendship!
ATTICUS: That *is* heart-filling, Colin. Frances?
FRANCES: I have never yet been able to read *Sordello*, but a favourite passage of mine comes from it. I met it in a book of

[1] *P.L.* vi. 712.

Miss Thackeray's and I often say it over to myself. I don't always get the lines right, because of an internal rhyme, and then I look it up again:

> a footfall there
> Suffices to upturn to the warm air
> Rich germinating spices. Mere decay
> Produces richer life, and, day by day,
> New pollen on the lily-petal grows,
> And still more labyrinthine buds the rose.

ATTICUS: O dear! I shall never be able to snap at Browning again.

[*After which, the girl and young man make their adieux, and go away together.* SIBYLLA *and* ATTICUS *settle down at the chessboard.*]

SIBYLLA: Thank you, Atticus; you behaved beautifully.
ATTICUS: So did you all. And what a lot Mr. Saintsbury knows, doesn't he!
SIBYLLA: And what a lot his "W. P." doesn't say, does he!
ATTICUS: A very sweet nature, I thought.

# III

# 'SAY NOT, THE STRUGGLE NOUGHT AVAILETH'

## By A. L. P. NORRINGTON

TO most of us Arthur Hugh Clough is a one-poem author. Indeed, his one poem that has passed into the common currency of the English Parnassus, and has the ring of immortal coinage, is known to thousands who could not name its author. 'Say not, the struggle nought availeth' is not only true poetry. There is in it a virtue, a power that deeply moves the English heart. It has been included in more than one collection of hymns, and has been quoted more than once in times of national peril, most memorably by Mr. Churchill on 27 April 1941, in a famous broadcast to America—'but westward, look, the land is bright'.

Those who to-day know more of Clough than this one celebrated poem, and two or three others that occasionally stray into anthologies, are few indeed, and only to be found among devoted readers of English poetry. In the first forty years after his death the collected edition of his poems, published by Macmillan, went through sixteen impressions, but there have only been four impressions since then, and the last (1920) has been out of print since 1932. There has been no volume of selections since Humphrey Milford's edition of 1910 (Clarendon Press), which has been out of print since 1925. Clough's name is now kept alive more by his commemoration in Matthew Arnold's beautiful but misleading *Thyrsis*, and by glowing references in nineteenth-century memoirs, than by the currency of his poems.

Yet he wrote, in addition to many shorter pieces, three long poems which are very readable, and contain some of the most fluent, dexterous, and assured writing of a poet who elsewhere sometimes repels the casual reader by a faltering earnestness. Two of these poems, *The Bothie of Tober-na-Vuolich* and *Amours de Voyage*, are, however, handicapped by being written in what Clough himself deprecatingly called 'Anglo-savage' accentual hexameters, a metre which, remote as it is from that of Homer or Virgil, yet falls most tunefully on ears accustomed to the poetry of Greece and Rome. The third poem, *Dipsychus*, shows Clough at the height of his powers, but the inspiration under which he began to write it in 1850 failed before the poem was worked into final form, and, good as the torso is, it is felt to be a torso.

*Dipsychus* was first printed in the collected edition of 1869, eight years after Clough's early death at the age of forty-two. The printed text is based upon a number of manuscripts, partly in note-books, partly on loose sheets, from which it was constructed by his widow with the help of J. A. Symonds and other friends. These manuscripts are still in existence. They were preserved by the family, among the rest of Clough's poetical remains, and are now in the possession of the poet's daughter, Miss B. A. Clough, through whose kindness I am enabled to write these notes.\*

About half the total bulk of Clough's poems were first published posthumously. Of the long poems, the *Bothie* appeared in 1848 and *Amours de Voyage* (serially, in the American *Atlantic Monthly*) in 1858. But *Dipsychus* and *Mari Magno* both lay in manuscript in 1861, unfinished. Of the shorter poems a mere handful were published in his lifetime. Some thirty appeared in *Ambarvalia*, a small volume of poems by Clough and his friend Thomas Burbidge which came out in 1849; a number of schoolboy poems were printed in the *Rugby Magazine* between 1835 and 1837; and one or two later poems were contributed to periodicals. The remainder, like *Dipsychus* and *Mari Magno*, were among his unpublished papers. Manuscripts of all, or almost all, survive. Among them is 'Say not, the struggle nought availeth'.

Of this poem there are no less than five surviving manuscripts in Clough's own hand. Three of them can be dated with certainty, and the position of the other two in the series can be demonstrated. No two of them are identical. Not one of them agrees precisely with the hitherto printed text.

---

\* I am also deeply indebted to Mr. Howard F. Lowry, President of Wooster College, Ohio, and formerly Professor of English Literature at Princeton University, whose researches into the text of Clough's poems are shortly to be published in the form of a definitive edition.

## 'SAY NOT, THE STRUGGLE NOUGHT AVAILETH'

It is possible that there was yet another manuscript which was used by Mrs. Clough as the basis of the text, but has disappeared. But it is improbable. There is no doubt that the surviving family collection of manuscripts was in fact the source of the text of many of the posthumous poems. Moreover, the latest of the five manuscripts of our poem, and the one that agrees most nearly with the printed text, occurs in a note-book containing fair copies of other poems, for whose printed text this note-book was almost certainly the source.

But let us examine the manuscripts one by one. The earliest is a rough draft in a thin demy 8vo ($8\frac{3}{4}$ in. × $5\frac{5}{8}$ in.) note-book in a brown paper cover. The contents of this plain little book are very miscellaneous, and very evocative. Two inscriptions on the outside—'Grasmere, L.V. '45' (L.V. no doubt stands for Long Vacation), and 'ROMA—MDCCCXLIX'—show two occasions when Clough made purposeful use of the book, but it was the receptacle of odd jottings on several other occasions.

The first twenty pages show how Clough spent his time at Grasmere in the summer of 1845. There are (apart from several blanks) nine pages of notes on political economy, four on miracles and redemption, and a light-hearted pencil sketch of naked bathers in a mountain-ringed lake, presumably Grasmere itself. The economic jottings are not uninteresting. They develop an argument in favour of something very like 'planning'. Clough had written the year before to his friend the Rev. J. P. Gell: 'I am considerably inclined just now to set to work at Political Economy . . . and to see if I cannot prove the Apostle of "anti-laissez-faire".' At Grasmere his ideas seem to have developed in favour of 'combinations' of enlightened political economists to settle in advance each year 'what the rate of wages and profit should be, independent of daily higgling'. But he was not sure. 'No doubt', he writes in the note-book, 'such combinations would require watching, as Railway Companies do. You might have a central board for this. But perhaps not.'

The next entry consists of two pages of notes (dated 31 December 1848) on immortality. And on the back of the second of these, facing the first page of a brief diary of his journey to Rome in 1849, is the draft of what was to become his best-known poem.

## 32 'SAY NOT, THE STRUGGLE NOUGHT AVAILETH'

The diary, which is very short, only a few words to each day, records his movements in France and Italy, especially the events of his stay in Rome from 16 April to 17 July. During this time he was an eyewitness of the siege by the French under Oudinot and of the defeat and downfall of Mazzini's shortlived Roman Republic, of which Mr. G. M. Trevelyan has written that 'there is no more moving incident in modern history'.\* The rest of the note-book is filled with drafts of poems: *Bethesda* and *Uranus*, fragments of *Amours de Voyage* and *Adam and Eve*, and two unpublished poems.

The draft of 'Say not', from its position in this note-book, from family tradition, and from the subject-matter of the poem, was clearly written when Clough was in Italy in 1849, and almost certainly at Rome. It is written in pencil (most of the contents of the book are written in ink), and in a very jerky hand, quite distinct from any other writing in the book. The conclusion is irresistible that Clough scribbled it down in circumstances unfavourable to steady writing, possibly in the dim light of dusk or dawn, perhaps with the note-book on his knee or propped on a ledge as he sat and watched the smoke of battle. On Sunday, 3 June, the fatal day of the French surprise attack which captured the Villa Orsini, the key to Rome, Clough's diary contains the entry: 'Battle fr. 4 a.m. to 9 p.m. forum by moonlight.' On 4 June he wrote to J. C. Shairp: 'They can't get in; they banged away by moonlight most of last night.'

Much of his time, during the four weeks of the siege, was occupied in watching the fighting, and the feelings of the foreign spectator (Clough himself was a warm supporter of the Italian patriots) are vividly described in *Amours de Voyage*:

Twelve o'clock, on the Pincian Hill, with lots of English,
Germans, Americans, French,—the Frenchmen, too, are protected,—
So we stand in the sun, but afraid of a probable shower;
So we stand and stare, and see, to the left of St. Peter's,
Smoke, from the cannon, white,—but that is at intervals only,—
Black, from a burning house, we suppose, by the Cavalleggieri;
And we believe we discern some lines of men descending
Down through the vineyard-slopes, and catch a bayonet gleaming.

On the Pincian Hill, then, or 'Montorio's height', or one of

---
\* *Garibaldi's Defence of the Roman Republic* (1907).

## 'SAY NOT, THE STRUGGLE NOUGHT AVAILETH'

the other vantage-points from which, during those hot and thundery June days, he watched Garibaldi's volunteers battling with Oudinot's regulars, Clough may have scribbled down the draft of his famous poem. Here it is, as far as print can reproduce the erasures and corrections and illegibilities of the pencilled page:

> Say not — the         nought availeth
>                 wounds
>   The labour & the ~~blood~~ are vain
>   The enemy faints not nor faileth
>   And as things have been things remain
> Though
> ~~If~~ hopes were dupes, fears may be liars
>   It may be, in yon smoke concealed
>   ~~Beyond that parting cloud hardby~~
> Een now │your comrades chase the flyers
>   And but for you
> Een now ~~upraise the victor cry~~
>        possess the       field
>       the tired waves
> For while ~~these billows~~ vainly breaking
>      here no
> Seem ~~scarce one~~ painful inch to win
> Behind  Far back    & inlets
> Thro creeks ~~its passage~~ making
>   Comes flooding   have the main ed
> The silent seas ~~come~~ flooding in
> Tis ~~And~~ not     ern
> ~~Nor is't~~ thro' east~~ward~~ windows only
>   When daylight comes, comes in the light
> In front the sun climbs slow how slowly
>         land
> Behind you, look the ~~field~~ is bright

If this, which I will call MS.[1], had been the only manuscript Clough left, the poem could have been printed very much as we know it. The fourth word of the first line would need to have been supplied. There would have been difficulties with l. 12. And there are other small differences, notably in the first two words of the last line. But we should not have lost much. Editorial punctuation would have been required, for, as so often in Clough's unfinished manuscripts, the draft contains almost none.

## 34 'SAY NOT, THE STRUGGLE NOUGHT AVAILETH'

At this point, to make what follows clearer, I give the poem as it appears in the last (MS.5) of the five manuscripts, and, below it, record the variations in MS.2, MS.3, MS.4, and the text as printed in 1862 (T):

> Say not the struggle nought availeth,
>   The labour and the wounds are vain,
>  The enemy faints not nor faileth
>   And as things have been, things remain.

⟨5⟩ If hopes were dupes, fears may be liars
   It may be in yon smoke concealed
  Your comrades chase e'en now the fliers
   And but for you possess the field.

  For while the tired waves vainly breaking
⟨10⟩  Seem here no painful inch to gain
  Far back through creeks and inlets making
   Came, silent, flooding-in, the main

  And not by eastern windows only,
   When daylight comes, comes-in the light
⟨15⟩ In front the sun climbs slow, how slowly,
   But westward, look, the land is bright.
1849. — Rome? —

MS.4 has a title *In Profundis*.
 1 not, MS.2, MS.3, T   'the MS.2
 2 vain; MS.3, MS.4
 3 not, nor faileth, MS.2, MS.3, MS.4, T
 4 been, things] been they T   remain.' MS.2
 5 If] Though MS.2   liars; MS.2, MS.4, T   liars, MS.3
 6 be, MS.2, T   concealed, T
 7 flyers, MS.2, MS.3   fliers, T
 8 Een now possess the peaceful field. MS.2   In MS.3 *incomplete after the first four words* E'en now possess the   And, but for you, T
 9 waves, vainly breaking, T
 10 painful] tedious MS.2
 11 back, ... making, T   inlets] MS.2 *has* eddies *erased and* inlets *written below*
 12 silent] noiseless MS.3, MS.4   Came silent flooding in the main. MS.2   Came, silent] Comes silent T
 13 'Tis not MS.3   MS.3 *and* MS.4 *omit comma after* only
 14 comes in MS.2, T   light, MS.4, T
 15 slowly! MS.3   MS.4 *omits comma after* slowly
 16 MS.2 *omits comma after* look   bright] light MS.3, *a slip of the pen*

**All other manuscripts omit date and place of composition.**

## 'SAY NOT, THE STRUGGLE NOUGHT AVAILETH'   35

After the pencilled draft, the earliest fair copy (MS.[2]) is in a letter written by Clough to the poet William Allingham on 13 October 1849, which came to light in 1941, when it was sold at auction at Sotheby's on 11 June. It was bought by the American publisher, Mr. Charles Scribner, for £75, and presented to Mr. Churchill.* The text is very close to that of MS.[5], already printed above. Apart from punctuation, it differs in three places only. In l. 5 the first word is 'Though' (as in MS.[1]). L. 8 reads 'Een now possess the peaceful field.' In l. 10 Clough wrote 'tedious' instead of 'painful', as in MS.[1] and in the three later manuscripts. He had another second thought in l. 11, where MS.[2] has 'eddies' crossed through and 'inlets' restored below. The punctuation is fuller than in MS.[5]; but there are no commas and no hyphen in l. 12, and no hyphen in l. 14.

The manuscript which I believe comes next in the series (MS.[3]) is a single sheet (10¼ in. × 7¼ in.), which was formerly among the family papers but was presented to Yale University Library in 1932.† On one side are the first fourteen lines of 'Say not', on the other the last two lines, followed by an unpublished sonnet beginning 'O'Brien, most disconsolate of men', which occurs also in the note-book containing MS.[1].

MS.[3] has no indication of date, and its place in the series can only be inferred from internal evidence. That it must be earlier than MS.[4] and MS.[5] seems clear from l. 8, which is incomplete after the words 'E'en now possess the', while MS.[4] and MS.[5] agree with each other, and with the printed text, 'And but for you possess the field'. The question is whether MS.[3] is earlier or later than MS.[2]. Verbally it is no closer than MS.[2] to MS.[5], as may be seen from the critical apparatus above (see ll. 5, 8, 10, 11, 12, 13). Nor is any sure clue afforded by variations in syntactical punctuation, which is casual in all manuscripts. But I believe that the evidence of the hyphens in ll. 12 and 14 ('flooding-in' and 'comes-in') is decisive. These hyphens occur in MS.[3], MS.[4], and MS.[5], but not in MS.[1] or MS.[2]. They have never been printed by Clough's editors, but

---

\* See the account by Mr. John Carter in the *Publishers' Weekly*, 2 Aug. 1941, pp. 309 ff.

† Grateful acknowledgement is made to Yale University for permission to quote this manuscript.

they have an important metrical significance, and are not to be disregarded, though perhaps they need not be printed.

Clough's bold and original handling of the hexameter in the *Bothie* and *Amours de Voyage* shows that he was ahead of his contemporaries in his understanding of the part played in English prosody by accent, or stress. The best account of the matter is Humphrey Milford's in his Introduction to his *Poems of Clough* (1910). He there quotes, and comments on, a note by Conington (from his *Life and Letters*) of a conversation with Clough in the autumn of 1848 (the year in which the *Bothie* appeared):

'His *Bothie* was just about to be published, and he gave me some account of it, particularly of the metre. He repeated, in his melodious way, several lines, intended to show me how a verse might be read so that one syllable should take up the time of two, or, conversely, two of one. The line which he instanced (altered, I think, from *Evangeline*) was this:—

White | naked | feet on the | gleaming | floor of her | chamber.

This was new to me, as I had not risen beyond the common notion of spondees, dactyls, and the rest.' An admirable accentual analysis of the first line of *Paradise Lost* follows; and if it were not for a doubt, expressly raised by Conington himself, whether his recollection of a twenty-years old conversation may not be tinged by his own 'subsequent use of the clue' then first given him, it would seem that Clough 'knew what he was doing' more than Mr. Bridges allows,* though he did not always do it.

To return to our hyphens, Clough's reason for inserting them, without fail, in MS.³, MS.⁴, and MS.⁵ was to guard against any wooden, time-beating tendency on the reader's part to place a stress on the word 'in'. He knew that his contemporaries, having labelled the metre of his poem as iambic, might try to stress the second syllable of each foot. L. 12, read thus, would become

    Came sí | lent floód | ing ín | the maín†

and l. 14

    When dáy | light cómes, | comes ín | the líght.

* 'If Clough did not quite know what he was doing in the versification ... yet he of all men most certainly knew what he was not doing' (*Milton's Prosody*, p. 106, note).

† MS.³ and MS.⁴ have 'noiseless' for 'silent', but this does not affect the argument.

## 'SAY NOT, THE STRUGGLE NOUGHT AVAILETH' 37

Clough intended a less rigid, and much more natural, distribution of stress, and he marked his intention by the hyphens, and in l. 12 by the extra commas, all of which had been missing in MS.², but were inserted in MS.³, MS.⁴, and MS.⁵. L. 12 is to be read with a stress on 'Came' (indicated by the comma placed after it), as well as on the first syllable of 'silent' (or 'noiseless'), and 'flooding-in' is to be read as if it were a single word of three rather rapid syllables with a slight stress on the first. The metrical effect is well matched to the meaning, as of the gentle, pulsing, but irresistible invasion of the tide:

Cáme, | sílent, | flooding-in, | the maín.

So much for MS.³, which thus appears from internal evidence to have been written some time between MS.² (October 1849) and the next two manuscripts to be considered, both written a year or more later. MS.⁴ and MS.⁵ occur in note-books containing fair copies of various poems written out by Clough for his friends. The note-book containing MS.⁴ was used after Clough's visit to Venice in 1850, for one piece in it (afterwards incorporated in *Dipsychus*) is headed 'At the exhibition of modern painting in the Academy at Venice', with the date '1850' added, apparently later. Various corrections, in Clough's hand, may have been made some time later, but the book was first written in before the note-book containing MS.⁵. Both books contain the poem *Lamech*, and a comparison of the two versions proves that that in the MS.⁴ note-book is the earlier. And there are other corroborative indications.

MS.⁴ is almost identical with MS.⁵. Apart from six differences of punctuation which prove nothing, the only verbal variant is 'noiseless' for 'silent' in l. 12. MS.⁴ is unique in having a title, *In Profundis*.

And now we come at last to MS.⁵, the text of which is printed above (p. 34). This manuscript is in a note-book containing fair copies of ten poems in Clough's hand and one (*Alteram Partem*) in another hand, evidently added later. It is inscribed on the first page as follows: 'Written out for B.M.S.S. April 1852. (τὰ ὀπίσω—).' The initials were Miss Blanche Smith's, to whom Clough became engaged early in 1852, and the book was made for her in the month in which his duties as Principal of University Hall, London, came to an end. They were married in 1854.

This 1852 note-book is the most carefully written of the surviving documents. There are not more than two or three corrections throughout. To each poem Clough appended a date (the dates range from February 1849 to April 1852), and generally also the place of composition. In every case the printed text follows this note-book very closely, and more closely than any other manuscript. In every case the notebook contains the latest surviving manuscript known, in four cases the only complete fair copy, and in one the only manuscript of any kind. There are good grounds for believing that this book was used by Mrs. Clough and her fellow editors as the basis of the printed text of the poems it contains.

But, if so, why does the printed text of 'Say not' (in addition to supplying some missing marks of punctuation) differ verbally from the manuscript in two places?

In l. 4 the text has

> And as things have been they remain

while MS.[5] has

> And as things have been, things remain

and in l. 12 the text has 'Comes' while MS.[5] has 'Came'.

It is of course possible that the text is derived from Clough himself. He may have spoken it so to his wife or to his friends, or he may have written it so in some manuscript which has disappeared. 'Say not' was among the sixty shorter poems which he himself planned to issue in a volume that was to contain also a revised text of the *Bothie*. He had spent the years 1852 and 1853 in America, and had made many friends. These friends, especially Charles Eliot Norton of Harvard, with whom Clough kept up an active correspondence till the end of his life, were constantly urging him to collect and publish his poems, and it was through their enthusiasm that *Amours de Voyage* appeared in the *Atlantic Monthly* in 1858. On 25 October 1860 Clough wrote to Norton: 'I have just sent off the corrected "Bothie", and two copies of all the little poems.' His directions for the arrangement of this proposed volume may still be seen

## 'SAY NOT, THE STRUGGLE NOUGHT AVAILETH'

among the Norton papers in Harvard Library, and were followed with very few changes in the simultaneous American (Ticknor and Fields, Boston) and English (Macmillan) editions of 1862.

At first sight it certainly looks, from this, as if there may have been separate copies of these short poems, and therefore of 'Say not', in addition to those that still survive in the family papers. But if so, why are they not among the Norton papers at Harvard, which contain other more trivial Clough manuscripts? The answer may be that they were returned to Mrs. Clough, who asked Norton more than once to return them, and in March 1862 wrote thanking him for 'the copies of the poems'. He certainly returned the corrected copy of the *Bothie*, but that is still among the family papers.

Whatever the truth of the matter, the strength of the manuscript support for MS.[5], the evidence from other poems, and from a statement by Mrs. Clough herself, that the printed text sometimes departs from its manuscript source, and, not least, the nature of the two variant readings that we are considering, leads me to believe that they are due to the editors—or possibly to the printers—and that the correct way to print these two lines is to follow MS.[5].

Let us examine these three arguments in turn. First, the manuscript support for MS.[5] is almost unanimous. In l. 4 all manuscripts, including the early draft MS.[1], read 'things remain', and all except MS.[1] have a comma before 'things'. In l. 12 all, except MS.[1], have 'Came'. In MS.[3] Clough actually wrote 'Come' (which is ungrammatical) and altered it by a pen stroke to 'Came'. In MS.[1] (see p. 33 above) he first wrote 'The silent seas come flooding in', and then wrote above the beginning of the line, 'Comes flooding', which shows that he first intended the more natural present tense. But he also (the line was never tidied up in this early draft) altered 'come flooding in' to 'have flooded in', a change from present to perfect.

Secondly, there is evidence that in dealing with Clough's unpublished manuscripts the editors sometimes emended the text. They were, indeed, obliged to do this in some poems where the manuscripts were unfinished, if they were to produce a text that made sense and scanned. But they went farther. There are in many poems variations between the printed text and the surviving manuscripts—manuscripts complete in sound and sense—which can only be explained on one of two hypotheses: (1) that there exist, or did exist, other manuscripts which support the text; or (2) that the existing manuscripts are indeed the only source of the text, but that the text departs from them deliberately, or by inadvertence.

Even if we had no positive evidence of emendation by the editors, the former hypothesis would be difficult to sustain. Why should Mrs. Clough have kept so carefully, and handed down to her children, a whole collection of inferior manuscripts and allowed the better manuscripts to disappear? And we know, from her correspondence with Norton between her husband's death in 1861 and the appearance of the first collected edition of his poems in 1862, that Clough left no series of 'authoritative' versions of even his most cherished poems. The editors had to use their judgement in producing the best text they could from the existing manuscripts. It seems impossible to doubt that, at any rate for most of the poems, the manuscripts now belonging to Miss B. A. Clough are those that were used by the editors in preparing the posthumous editions.

But it so happens that we have positive evidence of the editors' attitude towards emendation, from Mrs. Clough's correspondence with Norton, already mentioned. The plan was to make the American and English editions of 1862 simultaneous and as nearly identical as possible. Mrs. Clough expected to make corrections when she saw Macmillan's proofs, and she insisted that these corrections must be followed by the Boston printers. She wrote to Norton on 10 April 1862: 'I hear that Macmillan is in communication with Messrs. Ticknor and Fields, so I suppose it is arranged about the interchange of proofs. I fear it will make a very considerable delay, but there can be no other way of getting the two editions alike, for I expect there will be several alterations when the new poems are tried in print.' This can only mean one thing. She was contemplating the need to make editorial alterations in the poems now being printed for the first time. This is no proof that any alterations were actually made in 'Say not', but it shows that alterations could have been made.

Lastly, there is the evidence of the variant readings themselves. Granted that the readings in the text could be due to the editors, do they look like editorial emendations? Which is Clough more likely to have written? These are highly subjective questions. My own feeling is that in both places the manuscript reading is better poetry, and the printed text is more natural prose.

In l. 4 'they' might possibly be a simple misreading of 'things'. The words, though distinct, are not dissimilar in Clough's handwriting. Metrically 'things' is surely better than 'they'. The grammatically unnecessary but metrically significant hyphens that Clough inserted (and his editors omitted?) in ll. 12 and 14 show that he composed this poem with more than ordinary attention to stresses. The printed version of l. 4 substitutes a weak for a strong syllable in a line already weak in stresses. The effect of the change is to produce, perhaps, more natural prose, but it mars the music of the verse.

In l. 12 the alteration from 'Came' to 'Comes' is not merely natural, but may have seemed to the editors to be demanded by the normal practice of English syntax. 'Seem' in l. 10 demands 'Comes' in l. 12, or, if we retain 'Came', then we must read 'Seemed' in l. 10. Otherwise the sequence of tenses is broken. But, after his first draft, Clough wrote 'Came' in four successive copies. That he meant to write 'Came' is all the more probable because it is less natural than 'Comes'. He *may* have overlooked the lack of correspondence between the tenses. More probably he wrote what he wrote deliberately. He wished to convey the idea that while the waves continue to break vainly here, the main has already come flooding-in, an accomplished fact, not an action now beginning. Whatever the sense, 'Came' is to my ears more musical than 'Comes'.

Clough might have been gratified, he would certainly have been astonished, that the text of his poem should be so minutely discussed almost a century after it was first written down. He worked over this poem with uncommon care, but he never saw it in print; and he was always modest about his own writings. The last four lines of *Amours de Voyage* might have been his *requiem* for it:

Say, 'I am flitting about many years from brain unto brain of
    Feeble and restless youths born to inglorious days:
But,' so finish the word, 'I was writ in a Roman chamber,
    When from Janiculan heights thundered the cannon of France'.

# IV
# THE POETRY OF R. L. STEVENSON
### *By* H. W. GARROD

'THE peculiarity of Mr. Stevenson, among the set with whom he moved most when in London, was' (says one of the 'set') 'that he had never published verses.'[1] He was thirty-six when he ceased to be 'peculiar', and published *A Child's Garden of Verses*. The 'set' did not quite know what to make of it. But one of them at least was honest and gentlemanly about it. 'I could never read the book', says Lang, 'without a great inclination to cry.'[1] At a later date Lang spoke disparagingly of Stevenson's poetry. 'I do not think', he writes, 'that if he had written verse alone, his place would have been highly distinguished.'[2] Lang kept, even so, his old love for the *Child's Garden*—'a little masterpiece', he calls it, 'in a *genre* of Stevenson's own invention'.

For the secondary account in which the poetry of Stevenson is held, Lang, I fancy, has some responsibility. Yet the real mischief began, perhaps, with Stevenson himself. Stevenson practised self-depreciation as an art; and it is an art which no poet can afford. Freely and gaily in his Letters he applies to himself such terms as 'poetaster'[3] and 'prosator'.[4] 'You know my own description of myself', he writes to Colvin, 'as a person with a poetic character and no poetic talent.'[5] And 'a weak brother in verse', he calls himself in a letter to Henley.[6] 'Damned bad lines'[7] and 'doggerel'[8] he says of some excellent octosyllables that he has written; and of the *Ballads*, 'I don't know whether they are poetry.'[8] But when the *Ballads* failed with the public, it surprised him. 'I wondered', he says. Yet adds immediately: 'Not that I set much account by my verses.'[9] In reading these

---

[1] *A Child's Garden of Verses*, edited with an Introduction by Andrew Lang, 1907, pp. viii–ix.
[2] *Works of R. L. Stevenson*, Swanston edition, i. lii (my references to the *Works* are, throughout, to this edition).   [3] *Works*, xxiv. 396.
[4] Ibid. xxv. 58.   [5] Ibid. xxiii. 143.
[6] Ibid. 223.   [7] Ibid. xxiv. 172.
[8] Ibid. 186.   [9] Ibid. xxv. 58.

self-depreciations we must remember, I think, what Lang too much remembered, and what Stevenson himself could not but know, that the poet of *Underwoods* had, before *Underwoods* appeared, a distinguished repute in a different kind. The 'gratifying success', as he calls it, of *Underwoods* was, he knew, a success of the author of *Prince Otto* and of *Dr. Jekyll*. It was the success, again, of an author already successful in yet another department, the essay—*Virginibus Puerisque* and *Familiar Studies* had already found, if not a public, yet devotees. Accordingly, 'I do not set up to be a poet, only an all-round literary man; a man who talks, not one who sings.'[1] If *Underwoods* has merits, they are, at best, 'prose-merits'.[2] 'The verses are sane: that is their strong point, and it seems strong enough to carry them.'[2] For the *Ballads*, he is content to claim that they are the work of a man who can tell a story.[3] 'I don't know if they are poetry,' he writes, 'but they're good narrative, or I'm deceived.'[4]

'The true business of literature', he says, in the essay on Thoreau,[4] 'is with narrative. . . . There alone that art enjoys all its advantages, and suffers least from its defects.' In the Letters, similarly, he speaks of narrative as 'the most characteristic mood' of literature. The *Ballads* were a failure. He persuaded himself, even so, I think, that a poetry which stops this side of narrative wants nature and ultimate greatness. That, till the other day, was a truism of criticism. The 'grand poem' was the epic. That this truism should appear particularly true to Stevenson has a natural look; for he was primarily a novelist. Yet there was, in fact, something rather specially unnatural in it. For if, to-day, the epic, the verse-story, is dead, at least we know what killed it. It was killed by the novel. Beyond hope of resurrection, it was killed by Scott. A single edition of *Harold the Dauntless* satisfied, in 1817, a public which had exhausted seven editions of *Waverley*.

The greatest of the poetic kinds, the narrative kind, died from the novel, the novel of the early nineteenth century. The lyric kind still lived. But bore, even so, a threatened life. Here, too, the novel had killing power. When Stevenson says that

---

[1] Ibid. xxiv. 255.   [2] Ibid. 239.   [3] Ibid. xxv. 58.   [4] Ibid. xxiv. 395.

he does not 'set up to be a poet', that he is only 'a man who talks, not one who sings', he is thinking of the lyric kind. In this kind he allows himself 'prose-merits'. In truth, there was coming upon lyric, or at any rate upon the diction of lyric, a change of which the meaning and direction is still uncertain. It might plausibly be conceived—and for his own poetry Stevenson, with his insistent gift of self-depreciation, likes so to conceive it—as a change from singing to talking. Wordsworth had done something to kill poetic diction, and to bring into poetry 'prose-merits'. Yet poetic diction is preposterously like Nature; you may expel it with a pitchfork, but it keeps running back. If to-day we see very little of it, we owe thanks, I must believe, to the novel. It can hardly, I think, be accident that the three Victorian poets who wrought the disintegration of Victorian poetic diction were all of them novelists. The greatest of them I take to be Stevenson. But 'prosators' they are, all of them.

The first great poetic happening in Stevenson's life was when, as a boy, he read Swinburne's *Poems and Ballads*. Five-and-twenty years later he speaks feelingly of the 'spell' which the book cast over him.[1] How long the spell held him it is difficult to say—I do not know what inference can be drawn from the circumstance that, somewhere about the year 1876, he offered to a clerk in the railway booking-office a copy of Swinburne's *Queen Mother and Rosamond*, in part-payment of his fare to Edinburgh. When he wrote Poem xlix of the *New Poems*, he was plainly out of love with Swinburne; the only 'true poetic kin' then were Wordsworth and Burns, and he throws his Swinburne into the river.

The second great poetic happening came ten years after *Poems and Ballads*, when he fell upon Meredith's *Love in the Valley*. 'It got me,' he writes, 'I wept; I remembered that poetry existed'[2]—Swinburne, perhaps, had helped him to forget that. He was at Hyères, busy with his *Child's Garden of Verses*. 'The stanzas beginning "When her mother tends her" haunted me and made me drunk like wine.'[1] The very title haunted him. For it was there and then, I have always suspected, that he wrote, not for the *Child's Garden*, but for some

---

[1] *Works*, xxv. 390.   [2] Ibid. xxiv. 54; cf. xxv. 214.

undefined context, the lines printed in 1890 as Rua's Song in the *Feast of Famine*:

> Night, night it is, night upon the palms.
> Night, night it is, the land-wind has blown.
> Starry, starry night, over deep and height,
> Love, *love in the valley*, love all alone.

The *Child's Garden* was published in 1885, when Stevenson was living at Bournemouth. From Bournemouth he saw through the press his second venture in poetry, *Underwoods*. It was in Bournemouth, and at this time, that Sir Percy and Lady Shelley 'saw in his ways and character' 'a living image' of Shelley.[1] And not they alone. Reading, in 1887, Dowden's *Life of Shelley*, 'I am weary', Stevenson writes[2] to a friend of Lady Shelley's, 'I am weary of my resemblances to Shelley; I seem but a Shelley with less oil, and no genius.' By 'less oil' he means, I suppose, an inferior facility.[3] And the 'no genius' need not bother us—in a poet everywhere insistent to deny himself genius in poetry. To his Bournemouth friends he was always 'a winged creature', whom they expected, any day of the week, to 'vanish into the uttermost isle'.[4]

He had been reading Dowden's *Life*; and from some of his comments I should infer that he had been reading Matthew Arnold's review of it. Only once in his Letters does he mention Arnold—a casual reference to Arnold's 'Philistines', which might have come from someone who had not read him at all. But if I had to guess which of the great Victorians influenced Stevenson the most deeply, I should hazard Arnold. Somewhere, without naming him, he speaks of Arnold's dictum that conduct is three-fourths of life. Some people, he says, think that that is putting it too high. But the ethical prepossession is as strong with Stevenson as with Arnold himself. Stevenson's religion, I have often thought, was taken from him by Herbert Spencer—how strange to-day ring his iterated laudations of Spencer—and given back to him by Matthew Arnold. He took from Matthew Arnold, I suspect, his religion.

---

[1] Ibid. xxiv. 177.   [2] Ibid. 212.
[3] See *New Poems*, xxxviii. stanza viii. 1–2:
> Some song that shall be *suppling oil*
> To weary muscles strained with toil.

[4] *Works*, xxiv. 272.

More certainly, and more relevantly, he took from him his blank verse. I am bold to say that it is the best part of his poetry.

> Now things there are that, upon him who sees,
> A strong vocation lay; and strains there are
> That whoso hears shall hear for evermore.
> For evermore thou hear'st immortal Pan
> And those melodious godheads, ever young
> And ever quiring, on the mountains old.
> What was this earth, child of the gods, to thee?
> Forth from thy dreamland thou, a dreamer, cam'st,
> And in thine ears the olden music rang,
> And in thy mind the doings of the dead,
> And those heroic ages long forgot.
> To a so fallen earth, alas! too late,
> Alas! in evil days, thy steps return,
> To list at noon for nightingales, to grow
> A dweller on the beach till Argo come
> That came long since, a lingerer by the pool
> Where that desired angel bathes no more.

Lecturing on Stevenson's poetry some twenty years ago, I quoted that passage 'because the movement of it' (I said) 'owes something to Matthew Arnold'.[1] With it I quoted a poem 'somewhat more individual'—the lines beginning 'Not yet, my soul, these friendly fields desert'.[2] With that poem I might properly have quoted a poem which has the same occasion, an occasion fearful for any less soul than Stevenson's—for both pieces came from a sickness well-nigh mortal. The lines are addressed to Sidney Colvin, but his name is not given, and Stevenson could not bring himself to print the piece, because it was too personal—it was reserved for the posthumous *Songs of Travel*:[3]

> I knew thee strong and quiet like the hills;
> I knew thee apt to pity, brave to endure:
> In peace or war a Roman full equipt;
> And just I knew thee, like the fabled kings
> Who by the lone seashore gave judgment forth,
> From dawn to eve, bearded and few of words.

---

[1] *The Profession of Poetry*, pp. 187-8.   [2] *Underwoods*, xxiv.   [3] xix.

## THE POETRY OF R. L. STEVENSON 47

What, what was I to honour thee? A child,
A youth in ardour but a child in strength,
Who after virtue's golden chariot-wheels
Runs ever panting, nor attains the goal.
So thought I, and was sorrowful at heart.

Since then my steps have visited that flood
Along whose shore the numerous footfalls cease,
The voices and the tears of life expire.
Thither the prints go down, the hero's way
Trod large upon the sand, the trembling maid's;
Nimrod that wound his trumpet in the wood,
And the poor dreaming child, hunter of flowers,
That here his hunting closes with the great:
So one and all go down, nor aught returns.

For thee, for us, the sacred river waits;
For me, the unworthy, thee, the perfect friend.
There Blame desists, there his unfaltering dogs
He from the chase recalls, and homeward rides;
Yet Praise and Love pass over and go in.
So when beside that margin I discard
My more than mortal weakness, and with thee
Through that still land unfearing I advance:
If then at all we keep the touch of joy,
Thou shalt rejoice to find me altered—I,
O Felix, to behold thee still unchanged.

That the three pieces I have noticed owe something in the movement of their verse to Matthew Arnold is, I think, obvious. About most of the blank verse of the time there is a sort of dishonest beauty which the blank verse of Arnold and of Stevenson escapes. These three poems I put in the forefront of Stevenson's achievement. Of the blank-verse lyric—a kind invented, I suppose, by Coleridge and Wordsworth—I count Stevenson, if for these three poems only, a supreme master. I could wish that he had essayed the kind oftener. *Underwoods* furnishes seven examples of it,[1] *Songs of Travel* another seven.[2] There are no failures in the kind; and one or two examples of it fall not much below the three grand successes. As not much below them I would place *To Old Familiars* and 'The tropics

---

[1] x, xv, xvi, xxv, xxviii, xxxiv, xxxviii.
[2] xix, xxxv–xxxvii, xli–xliii.

vanish . . .', the latter memorable if only for its concluding lines:

> The voice of generations dead
> Summons me, sitting distant, to arise,
> My numerous footsteps nimbly to retrace,
> And all mutation over, stretch me down
> In that denoted city of the dead.

The kind reappears in the posthumous *New Poems*. Of the eight examples[1] of it there preserved, two of the most interesting are marred by an imperfect text (like so many of the *New Poems*). Both of them are addressed to Stevenson's wife.[2] The longer of them is perhaps worth setting out in an improved text:

> Fixed is the doom; and to the last of years
> Teacher and taught, friend, lover, parent, child,
> Each walks, though near, yet separate; each beholds
> His dear ones shine beyond him like the stars.
> We also, love, for ever dwell apart;
> With cries approach, with cries behold the gulf,
> As two great eagles that do wheel in air
> Above a mountain, and with screams confer
> Ahead athwart the cedars. Yet the years
> Shall bring us ever nearer; day by day
> Endearing week by week, till death at last
> Dissolve the long divorce. By faith we love,
> Not knowledge, and by faith, though far removed,
> Dwell as in perfect nearness, heart to heart.
> We but excuse those things we merely are,
> And to our souls a brave deception cherish.
> As from unhappy war a man returns
> Unfearing, or the seaman from the deep;
> So from cool night and woodlands, to a feast
> May someone enter, and still breathe of dews,
> And in her eyes still wear the dusky night.

These blank-verse lyrics of his Stevenson, I suppose, would have called, not singing, but talking. One or two of them have, perhaps, a studied domesticity. But the best of them I

---

[1] cxiv, cxxxviii–cxxxix, cxlvi, clxxiii–clxxv, ccxi.

[2] cxxxix, clxxv. In clxxv there are two obvious misprints: *surround* for *surrounds* in l. 1, *heard* for *hear* in l. 4. In l. 9 there seems to be a *who* missing before *breathed*.

# THE POETRY OF R. L. STEVENSON

must think the best of Stevenson's poetry; the verse lofty, sensitive, Arnoldian.

The influence of Arnold may be traced elsewhere in Stevenson's poetry; but manifesting itself less happily. Among the *New Poems* I seem to myself to trace these less happy connexions in at least five poems. The first of them is the poem bearing the title *Airs of Diabelli*.

> Days of April, airs of Eden,
> How the glory died through golden hours,
> And the silent moon arising,
> How the boat drew homeward filled with flowers.
> Age and winter close us slowly in.
> Level river, cloudless heaven,
> Islanded reed-mazes, silver weirs;
> How the silent boat with silver
> Thread[ing] the inverted forest as she goes
> Broke the trembling green of mirrored trees,
> O remember, and remember
> How the berries hung in garlands.
> Still in the river see the shallop floats.
> Hark. Chimes the falling oar.
> Still in the mind
> Hark to the song of the past.

There the 'airs of Eden', echoing Arnold's

> Airs from the Eden of Youth
> Awake and stir in their souls,

prepare us for the effects succeeding. I am content to call the verses Arnoldish. But there are cognizable Tennysonisms. Some of the verses, de-Arnoldized, reappear in *Songs of Travel* xii ('We have loved of Yore'). Arnoldish with a difference, and with revolt, is *The Cruel Mistress*—lest you should not perceive it, 'Better be Falstaff than Obermann' it ends. Stevenson's preoccupation with Obermann is illustrated elsewhere; from the essay 'Old Mortality' we know that he owed this preoccupation in the first instance to Arnold. The preference for Falstaff is his own; and enduring. Upon *The Cruel Mistress* follow, in the *New Poems*, three pieces—*Storm, Stormy Nights,* and *Song at Dawn*—all written, surely, when Stevenson was fresh

E

from Arnold's *Strayed Reveller*. The concluding stanzas of *Song and Dawn* are instructive:

> I too rise and watch
> The healing fingers of dawn—
> I too drink from its eyes
> The unaccountable peace—
> I too drink and am satisfied
>                         as with food.
> Fain would I go
> Down by the winding crossroad by the trees,
> Where at the corner
>                  of the wet wood
> The blackbird in the early grey and stillness
> Wakes his first song.

So far, it is what I may call mere Arnold. But the final stanza brings in dissonant notes:

> Peace! who can make verses clink,
> Find ictus following surely after ictus,
> At such an hour as this, the heart
> Lies steeped and silent.
> O dreaming, leaning girl,
> Already are the sovereign hill-tops ruddy,
> Already the grey passes, the white streak
> Brightens above dark woodlands, Day begins.

There the first line is pure Stevenson; the second line anything in the world; the 'dreaming, leaning girl' of l. 4 impossible for Arnold. All these five poems, in truth, are mixed effects, Cobham and San Francisco oddly, often ludicrously, intermingled. But that this free verse, 'ictus following ictus' unpredictably, goes back to Arnold there can be no doubt. Arnold supposed himself to be following the Greeks. In fact, he was following Goethe. He knew neither where his free verse came from, nor whither it was going. It was going to the land of so many unconsidered freedoms—to come back a mere incompetence. In *New Poems* cxcii Stevenson exchanges the free verse of Arnold for that of Walt Whitman, not unsuccessfully.

That the free verse of Stevenson has influenced in any appreciable degree the later practice of free verse I think not likely. The *New Poems* have never enjoyed vogue; nor could most of them deserve it. I call attention to Stevenson's use of these irregular measures, not because the poems in which he employs them are good, or successful, but because they illustrate his debt to Arnold. That debt is more happily illustrated in his blank verse. But these poems, and a good many others of the *New Poems*, serve to remind us of what we might otherwise easily forget, that the poetry of Stevenson is beholden everywhere to the processes of a painful scholarship. Greek Stevenson had none; he read Homer only in translation. With the Latin poets he was better acquainted; not disdaining, even here, the 'crib'. Virgil moved him profoundly;[1] and from the *New Poems*[2] we discover, what we should not otherwise, perhaps, have divined, the degree to which Martial intrigued him. In the Letters Martial is but once mentioned—he is 'a very pretty poet', but even so, not so pretty a poet as Herrick.[3] Lang, I think, records somewhere that, like Byron, Stevenson 'hated Horace' at school. But the *New Poems* offer some of the best Horatian Alcaics in our language:

> Brave lads in olden musical centuries
> Sang, night by night, adorable choruses,
> Sat late by alehouse doors in April
> Chaunting a song as the moon was rising;
>
> Moon-seen and merry, under the trellises,
> Flush-faced they played with old polysyllables;
> Spring scents inspired, old wine diluted,
> Love and Apollo were there for chorus . . .
>
> Youth goes, and leaves behind him a prodigy—
> Songs sent from thee[4] afar from Venetian
> Sea-green lagunes, sea-paven highways,
> Dear to me here in my Alpine exile.

Less happy in the same metre, from the same collection, is the poem *Tales from Arabia*.[5] Another Horatian metre, the asclepiad, carries one of the real successes of *New Poems*:[6]

> Flower-god, god of the spring, beautiful, bountiful,
> Gold-dyed shield in the sky, lover of versicles . . .

The *New Poems* are, in truth, principally interesting in so far

---

[1] *Works*, xxiv. 186, 265.   [2] cxlvii, clxxviii–clxxix, cxcix–ccx.
[3] *Works*, xxiv. 208.   [4] H. F. Brown.   [5] cxv.   [6] cxix.

as they illustrate Stevenson's untiring quest of form in poetry. He took up the quest where he might; and he ended where he must. He began with the French—that his best acquaintance with literature was with the French, he owed to chance. But for the grace of God, I sometimes think, and Matthew Arnold, he might be, in poetry, with the Dobsons, the Langs, the Lockers, and the rest of 'Banville's rhyming devotees'. 'A long while ago', he writes to Locker (in 1886), 'I broke my heart to try and imitate your verses, and failed hopelessly. I saw some of the evidence the other day among my papers, and blushed to the heels.'[1] The evidences of which he speaks are, no doubt, the Rondels of *New Poems* lxxviii, and some half-dozen other pieces of similar conceit from the same book, the best of them the poem 'Love is the very heart of spring'.[2] He began where he might. When I say that he ended where he must, he ended, I mean, not with the Dobsons, Langs, and Lockers, with the 'set' of the Savile Club, but, as happens with Scots not rarely, he ended in 'natural notes'. 'Sing truer or no longer sing', he enjoins the Muse of *Underwoods*: 'One natural note recapture.'[3] Throughout that miscellany of misfits and misfires which constitutes the *New Poems* he is hunting 'natural notes'. The trouble of them was that, so often, they seemed to end, not in singing, but in talking; in verses that had 'prose-merits', but not in

> Songs with a lilt of words that seem
> To sing themselves.[4]

The 'prose-merits' had value, of course, beyond what he divined; merits of nature, displacing Victorian tinsel, showing up Tennysonism.

Of 'songs that sing themselves' Stevenson wrote, in fact, not many; in *Underwoods* none, in *Songs of Travel* not half a dozen— 'Over the sea to Skye' may be reckoned decisive song, and so too, perhaps, 'The infinite shining heavens . . .', 'Bright is the ring of words . . .' and 'Home no more home to me . . .'. But in music other than song, and in 'natural notes', these two volumes surely abound. Of the poems in Scotch which furnish an

---

[1] *Works*, xxiv. 208.    [2] lxxxiii.
[3] xxxi.    [4] *New Poems*, xxxviii.

appendix to *Underwoods* I confess myself not able to judge. Nor can I judge better the Scotch poems of *New Poems*—perhaps that is why I prefer them to most of the other pieces in that 'gallery of failures'. Most of them are in what we call the Burns metre; where it is hard for a Scotchman to fail. How well Stevenson could use that metre in English is shown by the stanzas to R. A. M. Stevenson—'Not thine where marble-still and white . . .'.[1] But not judging what I cannot pretend to judge, I think myself to find in *Underwoods* and *Songs of Travel* lyric pieces which for nature, feeling, verse, words, challenge comparison with the best in our tongue. Not a few failures there are—fewer in *Underwoods* than in *Songs of Travel*. From *Underwoods* I would wish away perhaps nine pieces;[2] from *Songs of Travel* the two longest pieces in it (xxxviii–ix) and some eight others.[3] But enough remains; not all of it perfect, but none of it to be spared. Of Stevenson's blank verse I have spoken already. A master of the blank-verse lyric, he is master also of a measure far more difficult, the most ancient of English measures, the rhymed octosyllabic. Whether he learned this measure also from Matthew Arnold, I would not like to say. The Victorians in general did not much affect it. Arnold had in it one or two of his best successes. Stevenson's best success in it is *Our Lady of the Snows*. When he wrote that, beyond a doubt, he had Arnold in mind. He had in mind a poem of Arnold's which he recalls elsewhere,[4] a poem handling in a different measure, and in a different, almost opposite, temper, the same theme—the *Stanzas from the Grande Chartreuse*. Here is Stevenson's poem in full:

> Out of the sun, out of the blast,
> Out of the world, alone I passed
> Across the moor and through the wood
> To where the monastery stood.

---

[1] Ibid. xxxviii.

[2] vi, ix, xxv, xxvi (belonging properly to the *Child's Garden*, but even so below standard), xxix, xxx, xxxvi–xxxvii, xxxix.

[3] xxi, xxiii, xxiv (though here, I should be sorry to lose the Browningesque concluding stanza), xxvii, xxxi, xxxiv, xl, xlvi.

[4] *Death; New Poems*, xxxiv. The way in which Stevenson echoes Arnold may be illustrated even from his prose-works. In the first chapter of *The Wrecker* the mountains are said to 'break down in cliffs' (*Works*, xiii. 6). I cannot but think that Stevenson recalled, when he wrote that, Arnold's 'Where Helicon *breaks down in cliffs* to the sea'.

There neither lute nor breathing fife,
Nor rumour of the world of life,
Nor confidences low and dear,
Shall strike the meditative ear.
Aloof, unhelpful, and unkind,
The prisoners of the iron mind,
Where nothing speaks except the bell,
The unfraternal brethren dwell.

Poor passionate men, still clothed afresh
With agonising folds of flesh;
Whom the clear eyes solicit still
To some bold output of the will,
While fairy Fancy far before
And musing Memory-Hold-the-door
Now to heroic death invite
And now uncurtain fresh delight:
O, little boots it thus to dwell
On the remote unneighboured hill!

O to be up and doing, O
Unfearing and unshamed to go
In all the uproar and the press
About my human business!
My undissuaded heart I hear
Whisper courage in my ear.
With voiceless calls the ancient earth
Summons me to a daily birth.
Thou, O my love, ye, O my friends—
The gist of life, the end of ends—
To laugh, to love, to live, to die,
Ye call me by the ear and eye!

Forth from the casement, on the plain
Where honour has the world to gain,
Pour forth and bravely do your part,
O knights of the unshielded heart,
Forth and for ever forward!—out
From prudent turret and redoubt,
And in the mellay charge amain,
To fall and yet to rise again!
Captive? ah, still to honour bright,
A captive soldier of the right!
Or free and fighting, good with ill?
Unconquering but unconquered still!

And ye, O brethren, what if God,
When from Heaven's top he spies abroad,
And sees on this tormented stage
The noble war of mankind rage:
What if His vivifying eye,
O monks, should pass your corner by?
For still the Lord is Lord of might;
In deeds, in deeds, He takes delight;
The plough, the spear, the laden barks,
The field, the founded city, marks;
He marks the smiler of the streets,
The singer upon garden seats;
He sees the climber in the rocks;
To Him, the shepherd folds his flocks.

For those he loves that underprop
With daily virtues Heaven's top
And bear the falling sky with ease,
Unfrowning caryatides.
Those He approves that ply the trade,
That rock the child, that wed the maid,
That with weak virtues, weaker hands,
Sow gladness on the peopled lands,
And still with laughter, song and shout,
Spin the great wheel of earth about.

But ye!—O ye who linger still
Here in your fortress on the hill,
With placid face, with tranquil breath,
The unsought volunteers of death,
Our cheerful General on high
With careless looks may pass you by.

Stevenson uses the octosyllabic measure to different, but happy, effects, more than once in the familiar epistle. Examples are the poems to Will H. Low, H. F. Brown, and Andrew Lang.[1] I call attention to these letters to friends because a good deal of Stevenson's best poetry is written to, or for, friends; and of all our poets he may fairly be claimed as the most *friendly*. Some of the poems *to* friends fetch a poignant quality from the circumstance that they are written either from a sick-bed or from the other end of earth. No man was ever

[1] *Underwoods*, xi, xiii, xiv.

so much in love with life and with home as Stevenson, ever holding either by the slenderest of threads.

> Be it granted me to behold you again in dying,
> Hills of home.

Of poems that he wrote for friends, to the memory of friends, two stand out for their haunting music, and feeling unspoilt by thought: 'I knew a silver head . . .' and the verses for F. A. S. It must suffice to quote the second of them. It is addressed to Mrs. Sitwell (later Lady Colvin) whose memory will always be safe with readers of Stevenson, if only because he addressed to her letters which place him with the best of our letter-writers.

> Yet, O stricken heart, remember, O remember
> How of human days he lived the better part.
> April came to bloom and never dim December
> Breathed its killing dews upon the head or heart.
>
> Doomed to know not Winter, only Spring, a being
> Trod the flowery April blithely for a while,
> Took his fill of music, joy of thought and seeing,
> Came and stayed and went, nor ever ceased to smile.
>
> Came and stayed and went, and now when all is finished,
> You alone have crossed the melancholy stream,
> Yours the pang, but his, O his the undiminished
> Undecaying gladness, undeparted dream.
>
> All that life contains of torture, toil, and treason,
> Shame, dishonour, death, to him were but a name.
> Here, a boy, he dwelt through all the singing season,
> And ere the day of sorrow departed as he came.

For mere poetry, if I may so speak, that wants something. Critical ears, indeed, may deprecate a certain boyish quality that it has. That quality is, in truth, a part everywhere of Stevenson's mind and poetry. 'Always a child, always a boy', Lang calls him; adding, surprisingly perhaps—but Stevenson would have understood him—'like that other eternal boy, Shelley'.[1]

Whether boys still read Stevenson's novels, I do not know. But I know that I live surrounded by young men who read neither his novels nor his essays nor his Letters nor his poems.

---

[1] *A Child's Garden of Verses*, 1907, p. xii.

For myself, the novels, I confess, make a less appeal to me than they once did—excepting always *Prince Otto* and the first six chapters of *Weir of Hermiston*. The hold of the essays upon me I find greater than it was. The Letters I got to know only late; and I have never seen them adequately praised. If the Poems have anywhere been adequately praised, I do not know where it is. Fallen now upon neglect, they influenced deeply two poets who, till the other day, counted a good deal with the young—Housman and Rupert Brooke. But to-day, the young men about me no longer read Housman or Brooke— daily I hear both of them pooh-poohed. But I never allow myself to be discouraged; and when I am asked what poets we have had since Matthew Arnold, I say still always: Stevenson, Housman, Brooke. I think it would have disappointed Stevenson that young men should no longer read his poetry with pleasure; for he believed in youth, and waited upon its truth of judgement and temper. He did not 'set up to be a poet'. Yet in the best of what he had done in poetry he was conscious, I think, of some essential truthfulness and rightness, and looked to be remembered.

> Bright is the ring of words
>   When the right man rings them,
> Fair the fall of songs
>   When the singer sings them.
> Still they are carolled and said—
>   On wings they are carried—
> After the singer is dead
>   And the maker buried.
> Low as the singer lies
>   In the field of heather,
> Songs of his fashion bring
>   The swains together,
> And when the west is red
>   With the sunset embers,
> The lover lingers and sings
>   And the maid remembers.[1]

I cannot but think that when most of the poetry read to-day by young men is forgotten, some parts of the poetry of Stevenson will be still freshly and affectionately remembered.

---

[1] *Songs of Travel*, xv.

# V

## A POET IN WALTON STREET

### By SIMON NOWELL-SMITH

THROUGHOUT the fifty-seven years between his first book and his last Robert Bridges took an interest in the visual presentation of his work. His *Poems* of 1873 was published on commission by Basil Montagu Pickering, who was carrying on, though without the same flair, the tradition that had set William Pickering's work in the forefront of nineteenth-century English book design. Whether Bridges deliberately chose the Pickering firm for its long and happy association with the Whittinghams of the Chiswick Press is not recorded: but it is known that he took a personal interest in the layout of his first book and himself ordered the few copies that were printed on larger, hand-made paper, and it may well have been at his instance—though the Chiswick Press was a common choice of publishers of verse in the nineteenth century—that the Whittingham imprint reappeared on several of his later books and pamphlets in the next twenty years, some published by his friend Edward Bumpus and some by Bell. Of the three Bumpus–Whittingham pamphlets of *Poems by the author of 'The Growth of Love'*,[1] two show Bridges experimenting with different type-sizes for poems of different metres, and the third shows either the poet or the printer experimenting with tinted margins. Both Bumpus and Bell, however, like Blackwell in the same period, sent others of Bridges's books to other printers. The *Eight Plays*, 1885–94, for example, were printed by Clay; there is a tradition that their unusual and forbidding typography was intended as an improvement upon that more celebrated poetical part-issue in double-column, Browning's *Bells and Pomegranates*, 1841–6. Meanwhile Bridges's real apprenticeship as an amateur typographer was under Dr. Daniel. Mr. Holbrook Jackson has suggested[2] that Bridges influenced for the good both the taste and the technique of the Daniel Press: this is likely, but the

---

[1] Second series, 1879; third series, 1880; 'first series, second edition' (the last in order of publication), 1880.

[2] *The Printing of Books*, 1938, pp. 99 ff.

influence was reciprocal, for it was Daniel's good taste that had led him to acquire, five years before Bridges first sent him a poem to print in 1881, certain of the long-neglected Fell types to which the poet remained faithful (with some lapses) to the end of his life.

Before the early nineties, then, Bridges's published books bore a variety of printers' imprints. After the early nineties, until his death in 1930, it was exceptional for any published book of his to bear an imprint other than that of the printer to the University of Oxford—Horace Hart to 1915, John Johnson from 1925: Bridges had found a printing house to his own taste. From 1912 onwards only one volume of verse, two anthologies (one of them Oxford-printed), and one pamphlet (a B.B.C. copyright) bear the name of a publisher other than the Clarendon Press or, as publisher to the university, Henry Frowde or Humphrey Milford: a publishing house to his own taste had discovered Bridges.

The first separate production of Bridges to come from the Press was an anonymous 20-page offprint, privately circulated in 1887, of his contribution to Canon Beeching's edition of *Paradise Lost*, Book I, in the Clarendon Press Series. This is the earliest of a number of offprints pulled for him by the Press and the earliest hint of direct communication between author and university printer. Three years later his *Shorter Poems*, published in London by Bell, was printed in Oxford by Hart;[1] in 1892 his

[1] The bibliography of this edition is confused. It was first published (Books I–IV) in October 1890, with that year printed on the title-page and blocked on the three variant binding-cases of the small-paper copies. The 'second edition', a re-impression with a sentence added to the note on p. 87, was published in January 1891 and bears that year on the title-page; it has an undated paper label, instead of blocking, on the case. The 'third edition', published towards the end of 1891 and correctly dated on the title-page, is sometimes found in undated cases and sometimes in left-over first-impression cases dated 1890.

The 'fourth edition', with the addition of Book V, appeared in 1894. (Book V had already been separately printed by Daniel in 1893 and included in the same year in a volume printed, to secure copyright, in the U.S.A.; it was later offprinted by Hart from the 1894 Bell edition to complete the large-paper issue of 1890.) The 'fifth edition' appeared in 1896, the sixth and seventh, paper-wrappered and cheaper in price, in 1899; and it was thereafter frequently reprinted.

The second impression was NOT printed in November 1890, as Bridges's own bibliographical note in his *Collected Poems* has maintained from 1899 to the present day. Book V was NOT first included in 1896, as Bridges's note asserts, nor yet in 1899 as the anonymous bibliography published by Chaundy & Co., 1921, which Bridges revised, asserts. Incidentally the Chaundy bibliography was NOT compiled by Mr. Iolo A. Williams, as has often been stated (most authoritatively in the catalogue of the British Museum Library), but by Leslie Chaundy and E. H. M. Cox.

*Achilles in Scyros* was also printed for Bell by Hart; and in 1893-4 his *Milton's Prosody* was both printed and published by the Press. In 1895 the planning of the *Yattendon Hymnal* marks the beginning of active collaboration between Bridges and Hart. They combined for the hymnal both letterpress and music types which had been procured for the Sheldonian Press by Bishop Fell in the seventeenth century and of which the punches and matrices still survived in the foundry in Walton Street. The small pica roman and italic had already been used by Daniel for more than one of Bridges's books. The music was printed in four-line pica (48-point) types specially founded, with the aid of a hand-pump, from the long-disused matrices of Peter Walpergen: Bridges chose the face for 'this book ... offered in no antiquarian spirit' because, as he said, 'it was the only one that I could find of any beauty'. Hart was the printer: the real publisher, however, was not Frowde but Bridges himself. The cost of 200 copies in royal 4to, as of both the limited and unlimited editions of the word-book marketed by Blackwell, was to be borne by Bridges, and he hoped to meet it, at least in part, by the sale of a special issue, 'fifty copies in large size folio on the best paper. These ... were made out of compliment to the printer's workmanship and the beauty of the type.' The slow realization of this hope appears from a letter which Bridges wrote to Frowde as late as 1908: 'I should be glad if you could persuade any customers to buy the folio.' Whether or not copies had earlier been stored at the Oxford Warehouse, Amen Corner, as the imprint suggests, by 1908 the remaining stock was at Bridges's house at Chilswell, and when Frowde received an occasional order for a copy he had to apply to Bridges for it.[1]

The four parts of the hymnal were published in November 1895, June 1897, and January and December 1899. The interval of eighteen months between Parts I and II may have owed something to Bridges's preoccupation with another adventure in church music, *Yattendon 4-part Chants*, 1897. Again this was undertaken by Hart, at Bridges's expense, and again

[1] It does not seem to be on record that, while the original 4to *Hymnal* was specifically limited to 200 copies, Parts I and II were reprinted in this format. The reprints are readily distinguished by the absence of an upper-case note (present in the first impression) at the foot of Part I leaf F3 recto; and by the corrected printing of *Fraudis venena* (*venenam* in the first impression) *nesciat* in the fifth stanza of the Latin text on Part II leaf G4 recto.

in both folio and 4to; but it was privately printed, for the use of the Yattendon choir, and neither letterpress (apart from one preliminary leaf) nor music was typeset. The body of the book was photolithographed from a copy in which the musical notation was in Bridges's hand and the lettering in the hands of Mrs. Bridges and Lionel Muirhead. This is the first, but not the last, appearance of Mrs. Bridges as a calligraphic interpreter of her husband's work. In the second interval of eighteen months, between Parts II and III of the hymnal—an interval which saw the publication by the Press of Mrs. Bridges's *New Handwriting for Teachers*—Bridges began to prepare the text of the six-volume collected edition of his poetry and plays published by Smith, Elder in 1898–1905. It is significant of the poet's relations with his printer and publisher that he sent the copy for the first volume direct to Hart. The volume was printed in the same Fell fount as had been used for the hymnal.

His few separately published works between 1899 and 1912 throw little light upon Bridges's relations with the Press, though Hart's imprint continues to predominate. But there is light from another quarter. These were years given to testing 'Will Stone's versification' and, as a corollary to Stone's theories, to working out a system of phonetic spelling which, without looking outlandish or obscuring derivations, might help to fix syllabic quantities and to arrest the decay of English speech. Phonetic spelling led to phonetic script. Edward Johnston, a great calligrapher, was put under contribution: and in the Daniel Press edition of *Now in Wintry Delights*, 1903, Bridges included a facsimile, executed in collotype at the University Press, of 23 lines of the poem written out by himself in a phonetic adaptation of an eighth-century half-uncial script.[1] From phonetic script it was a short step to phonetic type. A fine roman and italic had been rescued from the Walton Street limbo for Daniel, and a music type of pre-eminent beauty for Bridges himself: why not also a fount suggesting—not indeed half-uncial, there was none—but at least some 'scribe's script' of reputable ancestry on which new characters might be grafted? Hart would know. And Hart did know. He dug up an early eighteenth-century anglo-saxon alphabet, one of two designed

---

[1] Bridges's manuscript of this, together with a manuscript of the whole poem in (more or less) normal spelling, is in Bodley, MS. Eng. poet. c. 22.

by that *erudita fæmina* Elizabeth Elstob; the matrices had been presented to the Press by the younger William Bowyer in 1753 and had not been used since. The gradual evolution of Elstob phonetic, a lower-case alphabet of 58 letters, diphthongs and ligatures, is too large a subject for discussion here: the surviving documents show the poet, his wife and the printer exchanging memoranda, drawings, proofs and personal visits at frequent intervals for a full two years before the new type was offered to public view in Bridges's contribution to the *Essays and Studies* of the English Association, 1910. The new Elstob characters were drawn by the erudite Mrs. Bridges.

In 1911 the Press printed and published 'perhaps the most satisfying of all the books which come under the typographical influence of Robert Bridges, ... an example of a perfect marriage between printing and authorship'[1]—Bridges's edition of the poems of his friend Digby Mackworth Dolben. Set in a modern-face type, it is certainly one of Horace Hart's triumphs. Then in October 1912, at the suggestion of a subordinate, Mr. Milford, Frowde included Bridges's own *Poetical Works, excluding the eight dramas,* among the single-volume Oxford Poets. He was the only living poet in the series; his inclusion made him for the first time, and the last time but one, a best-seller; and it perhaps helped to make him something more. 'M-milford,' he was able to say in the following summer, 'you've m-made me—L-laureate.'[2]

The success of the *Poetical Works* was not followed by any published book of original verse for eight years. Bridges's only book of verse in the interval was a small volume printed in a small edition by St. John Hornby at his Ashendene Press in 1914. His only published books, as distinct from pamphlets, during the war were an anthology, *The Spirit of Man,* printed by the Press for Longmans, 1916, and *Ibant Obscuri.* The latter consists of selected passages from the *Aeneid* and the *Iliad* with a line-for-line paraphrase in Bridges's quantitative hexameters and, for comparison, a cento of earlier English translations.

---

[1] Holbrook Jackson, op. cit., p. 108.

[2] Edward Thompson, *Robert Bridges,* 1944, p. 83. Thompson speaks of the transfer of Bridges's books to the Press at this date; in fact it was not until 1929 that John Murray, as successor to Smith, Elder, transferred the unsold stock of the six-volume *Poetical Works* of 1898–1905.

Because his versions were in the prosody out of which his phonetic alphabet had been born, his original intention was to print them in Elstob phonetic, and as early as 1910 a specimen page had been set up in that type. But Hart was now dead: the long and friendly collaboration to which Bridges pays tribute in the preface to *Ibant Obscuri* was ended; no longer could the author depend upon the 'patience and enthusiasm for typography' of the printer. The book was printed in 1916 by Frederick Hall, Hart's successor, in a variety of Fell founts (not altogether unadulterated), the older translations in small pica roman on the versos and Bridges's paraphrase on the rectos in the same size, interlined with the Latin and Greek originals in brevier roman and a correspondingly small greek.[1] The result is more readable than the phonetic specimen, partly because the anglo-saxon itself, even without the many idiosyncratic diphthongs and ligatures, is unfamiliar to the modern eye, and partly because Bridges has allowed himself comparatively few devices—hyphens, apostrophes, accents—to indicate his quantitative aims. But the cursive greek type, which with its 'picturesque ligatures' especially delighted Bridges,[2] is by reason of those ligatures distracting to the reader brought up on Oxford Classical Texts. The general appearance of a two-page opening with these varied sizes, variously leaded, with upper-and-lower-case italic head-lines, and with upper-case cross-heads ornamentally framed on the left-hand page, is remote from a 'perfect marriage between printing and authorship'.

In 1919 Bridges took up again a scheme which had been projected in 1913 and interrupted first by his appointment as Poet Laureate and then by the war. He launched the Society for Pure English. From the start the Press had lent him official and unofficial support. Hart, an original member, had printed the 1913 prospectus: Hart's successors have printed, and the Clarendon Press has published, all the *S.P.E. Tracts*. The first list of members of the revived society included Mr. Milford,

[1] In the greek type the height of the capitals and the lower-case $\pi$-height are approximately the same as those of the roman brevier, so that the value to the eye is identical. But a pica body is required to accommodate the accents and long ascenders and descenders of the greek.

[2] *Robert Bridges and the Oxford University Press* [by John Johnson, 1930, an exhibition display-label].

Publisher to the University, and Mr. R. W. Chapman, who was within a few months to become Secretary to the Delegates of the Press. Four years later Mr. Kenneth Sisam, the present Secretary, joined the committee. In 1925 Bridges wrote, with mingled gratitude and regret, that the only local centres of the society in the British Empire were the branch offices of the Press.[1] Running this 'private academy', writing some of its tracts, editing almost all (aided by Mrs. Bridges's 'beautiful penmanship, enthusiastic interest and clear and fine judgement'[2]) occupied the leisure hours of his last ten years. 'My vein of poetic activity has exhausted itself, I think. I must settle down to do some work for the S.P.E.' So he wrote to Logan Pearsall Smith[3] in the spring of 1922: he had recently in the space of a few months completed the core of the volume later published as *New Verse written in 1921*; a year earlier still he had published *October*.

For his first book of verse after the war Bridges left the Press which had printed almost all his published books—his own poetry and works of scholarship and his editions of his friends Dixon, Dolben and Hopkins—for nearly a quarter of a century. *October and Other Poems*, 1920, was printed by Billing of Guildford for William Heinemann: its type face recalls the Dolben volume of 1911, but its overweighted headings and the ungainliness of the page do not suggest Bridges's taste. The English edition, including a large-paper issue, consisted of 1,530 copies for sale: of these Heinemann failed to sell 153, which the Press took over for reissue with a cancel title-page nine years later.

*October* contained four poems in a new syllabic metre, the forerunner of the metre of *The Testament of Beauty*. Wishing to canvass his friends' opinions of his 'neo-Miltonic syllabics', in 1923 Bridges had a few copies of a fifth such experiment, *Poor Poll*, printed at the Press as a 4-page 4to leaflet in Fell english roman. In the summer of 1925 he began to prepare the collection called *New Verse*, which the Press was to publish; but meanwhile he had formed a high opinion of the typographic enterprise of Mr. Stanley Morison, adviser to the Lanston Monotype Corporation, and he agreed to allow his neo-Miltonic experiments, now twelve in number (four[4] from the *October* volume

---

[1] *S.P.E. Tract XXI*, 1925, p. 16.
[2] Logan Pearsall Smith, *S.P.E. Tract XXXV*, 1931, p. 499.  [3] Ibid., p. 501.
[4] One of the four, through an oversight, was omitted from Mr. Morison's book.

and eight destined for *New Verse*) to be used for the first presentation of Arrighi, a decorative sixteenth-century Italian cursive lately re-cut by Frederick Warde in close association with Mr. Morison. *The Tapestry*, 150 copies privately printed 'by F[rederick] W[arde] and S[tanley] M[orison]', appeared in November 1925. For the present survey the book holds two points of interest. Bridges prevailed upon Mr. Morison to design an additional character in order to distinguish soft from hard 'g'—a distinction which the harassed compositor, not surprisingly, sometimes overlooked. Secondly he insisted that Mr. Morison, as publisher, should 'write (that is sign)' the introductory note, just as later he was to insist that his note on the spelling of *The Testament of Beauty* should be given the appearance of having been written by the publisher. *New Verse*, delayed by a strike at the bindery, followed in December. Bridges wished this book, in both its limited and trade editions, to range in height with the smaller, crown 8vo, form of his one-volume *Poetical Works.* As the lines of the neo-Miltonics tended to be unusually long and he wished to avoid turning, he sought an unusually small type-face. A specimen was pulled in the Baskerville brevier which Daniel had successfully used for his miniature edition of Blake's *Songs*, 1885, but as this would have required hand-setting he chose, from the machine-types available at the Press, a standard revived old-style in the same size.

In Mr. Morison Bridges had found a printer who combined 'enthusiasm for typography' with invention and taste. When early in 1926 Mr. Milford, at Chilswell, suggested reprinting some of his prose writings, Bridges counter-proposed that he should be allowed to indulge his fancy for typographic innovation and that Mr. Morison should be invited to design the necessary phonetic characters—'one or two at most, to add to the "g"'. Tripartite negotiations followed. Their first, if subsidiary outcome was that one of the prose essays, on Shakespeare, was given to Mr. Morison to print privately in the United States: the American collectors' craze for limited editions was near its height and, besides his love of fine printing, Bridges did not scorn the chance of 'getting money from the Yankee to the Briton—we need it'. The larger project began to bear fruit in the autumn of 1927 when the Press published the first number of the *Collected Essays, Papers &c. of Robert Bridges*, with four phonetic symbols added to the ordinary lower-case alphabet. The type adopted was a recent Monotype recutting of another cursive, Blado, which had a family likeness to Arrighi but which, unlike Arrighi, was available for machine composition. Fresh symbols were added progressively. With the fourth number, the last that Bridges lived to edit, the Blado-*cum*-Chilswell alphabet had grown to thirty-nine characters, and after his death Mrs. Bridges brought up the total to fifty-four. The new symbols were cut in 13-point for the text and 10-point for the footnotes. For capitals Bridges desired no phonetic forms either in his Elstob adaptation or in Chilswell; a single size of Poliphilus roman was bigamously, and a little unhappily, married to the two sizes of lower-case italic. In the sixth number Mrs. Bridges, upon whom the chief burden of ensuring the accuracy of the printing had fallen, recorded her gratitude to the Press 'not only for their unfailing patience with the numerous revises demanded by the new type and spelling, but also for much friendly help and advice'.

When the idea of the *Collected Essays* was first broached in March 1926 Bridges was already at work upon a long new poem. By the end of the year he had written some 800 lines. It was to be a statement of his philosophy, if—he was in his eighty-third year—he should live to complete it. Seeing that he was discouraged and retarded by the physical labour of writing, rewriting and copying (though Mrs. Bridges could help him with the last), Mr. Sisam offered to put the draft, so far as it had then gone, into type in the style of the private print of *Poor Poll*. The poem had as yet no name. It was entered in the records of the Press as 'Philosophical Verse', with the order number 3328.[1] At Chilswell it became known as *De Hominum Natura* or, more familiarly, *D.H.N.* Of this first draft Bridges wished for at most twenty-five copies, some to keep to work on—as another writer might work on a typescript and a couple of 'carbons'—the others to circulate among discriminating friends. He was sent a proof in January 1927. The type was the large size used for *Poor Poll*, but well leaded; the margins, without ornamental

---

[1] This number appears on the signature leaves of the first eight impressions in 8vo of *The Testament of Beauty*. The details of the publishing history of the poem come mostly from the records of the Press, by kind permission of the Secretary to the Delegates.

border, appeared more generous; the paper was whiter and heavier; the whole effect more luxurious. Bridges remonstrated half-heartedly, but was clearly pleased at the magnificence which the Press had deemed appropriate to the *magnum opus* of his old age. On one point he was emphatic. 'You must not,' he wrote to Mr. Sisam, 'make a *publication* of this. I wish for no title, nor any press mark or indication of printer—merely date at end.' Twenty-five copies of Book I (and one or two 'overs') were printed in February 1927, with no title or imprint, and no date other than that of the completion of the writing, 'Dec. 24th, 1926'. The greater number of these were sent, for comment, to the poet's friends: if any friend failed to comment, and some did fail, the poet was displeased. Book II, completed in July 1927, was printed in September; Book III, completed in March 1928, was printed in May; and the first 1,135 lines of Book IV, completed in December 1928, were printed in February 1929. Of each part there were 25 copies. And still the poem had no name.

In the early stages, before the writing was finished, Bridges had no clear idea of the form which he wished the published edition, or editions, to take. In January 1927, while the draft of Book I was in proof, Mr. Sisam reported to Mr. Milford, 'He is not going to publish in England, but he thinks of letting Morison publish 100 copies in America'. Before the poem was completed there were signs that the bottom might soon drop out of the American limited-edition market, yet when publication became a practical issue, in the summer of 1929, Bridges still had that market in view: he wrote to Mr. Milford about 'the luxe edition' which he thought Mr. Morison might print in the United States and the trade edition which the Press would publish in Britain. The Press, however, was unwilling to forgo the prestige of publishing in both countries, and it was finally agreed that there should be three settings: a trade 8vo for Britain; a 4to *de luxe* designed by Mr. Morison but printed and published by the Press, also for Britain; and a collector's edition, printed in America and published by the New York branch of the Press. The British and American editions, Bridges announced in June, would have different titles: he had two in mind, was reluctant to sacrifice either, but would disclose neither. On the 26th of that month the revised copy of Book I of '3328—Bridges's Philosophical Verse' was received in Walton

Street; specimen pages were forthwith set up. On 8 July Mr. Sisam reported to Mr. Milford: 'Bridges has a great eye for a title. It is to be *The Testament of Beauty*.' A week later the final batch of copy was with the printer. A fortnight later again another surprise was sprung. Bridges announced that he intended to insert a dedication, but he was not yet prepared to disclose it.

The typography of the 8vo *Testament* was governed by the same considerations as *New Verse*, and after some experiment the same size of page and the same small size of type (8-point) were chosen. In the discussion of page, fount, leading, ornaments, dedication to the King—revealed at length in late September—and binding Mrs. Bridges played at least as active a part as Bridges himself, and it was she who undertook when sending the copy that it would be adequately punctuated: she did not normally, she explained, put stops in her transcripts of her husband's work because he never agreed with them, and he had not bothered to punctuate the private edition. First proofs were sent to Chilswell at intervals throughout August. The last batch included Sig. o (pp. 193–4), which does not appear in the finished book. This contained Bridges's note on his spelling, written as though by the publisher: its text varies in several places from that of the 4-page leaflet which, at the author's request, was finally tipped into the 8vo and inserted loose in the 4to. Bridges's care for the appearance of every page led him to alter in proof the spacing between certain paragraphs, so that it would be rash for any commentator to read a literary or philosophical implication into differences of spacing between the private and published texts. Mrs. Bridges designed the title-page and made a first drawing for the dedication. She wrote proposing for the binding-case a modified version of the imitation vellum of *New Verse*, 'without the fussy angle-fillings'; 'Testament' must be blocked in a single line, and 'Beauty' be no larger; between title and author's name the word 'by' must not appear.[1] The decision that the copy for the King, now in the library at Windsor Castle, should have its dedication in gold and be bound in real vellum was perhaps Bridges's own.

The final proofs of the 8vo were pulled between 24 August

---

[1] This injunction was not passed on to Mr. Morison, whose binding bears the forbidden word.

and 12 October. Publication was fixed for 24 October, the day after Bridges's eighty-fifth birthday. Meanwhile the 4to was being set, against time, from proofs of the 8vo as they became available. (Slight inconsistencies of proof-reading led to a few unimportant variants between the two texts.) Mr. Morison had had a free hand with the design. He tried a crown 4to page in 14-point Bembo roman, a new Monotype version of a fifteenth-century Venetian type; and a demy 4to page in the 16-point of the corresponding italic. Bridges preferred the roman and the larger page, and 16-point Bembo roman was decided upon. Eric Gill designed and cut the dedication, which was printed in an unusual, and unusually successful, shade of red. Both 8vo and 4to (50 signed and 200 unsigned copies) were ready, though in barely sufficient numbers to justify publication, on the appointed date.

On the day before, his birthday, Bridges received an unexpected gift. The private edition of his unnamed poem had broken off, as has been seen, in the middle of Book IV. With the decision to publish he required no working text of the conclusion, either for his own use or for the comments of his friends. Mr. Milford, Mr. Chapman and Mr. Sisam, however, decided to present to him a completion of the part-issue. Accordingly the text of Book IV, ll. 1136–end, was set up from an uncorrected proof of the 8vo, and four copies (and one or two 'overs') were printed in September 1929. One of these was given to Bridges. He asked that sufficient further copies should be printed to complete the sets which he had given away. Seventeen copies, therefore, differentiated in the colophon, were struck off in October. He wrote to Herbert Warren: 'The Press insisted on printing it (tho' it was of no possible use to me), in order to complete their magnificent setting up of the previous sections—which were an inestimable assistance to me in my work'. Only in the colophon of this fifth section does the name of the poem appear.

The American edition, like Mr. Morison's, was set from machine pulls of the English 8vo. It has no textual value. At an early stage the names of several printers were canvassed. Crosby Gaige was known to be anxious to print some work of Bridges's; Logan Pearsall Smith proposed Bruce Rogers; Mr. Cumberlege, head of the New York branch of the Press, at one point favoured D. B. Updike. Finally Mr. Cumberlege, with whom the decision rested, chose William Edwin Rudge, of Mount Vernon, and Rudge imported from England for the purpose a Linotype version, by George W. Jones, of one of the types of the great French bible printer of the sixteenth century, Robert Estienne. The first American printing, 250 copies in double crown 8vo, was published in December 1929; the second, a royal 8vo reduced photographically from the first, in January 1930.

Publication day in London found the Press unprepared for any great public demand for the 8vo. But the demand was made. Two thousand copies had been printed, and only a part of the impression bound. Next morning, 25 October, another 1,800 were ordered to be printed, but were sold out before delivery; on 31 October another 2,500 were ordered. Still the demand could not be met. With stocks running low at Amen House, paper ran out at Walton Street, and for the later impressions a different quality was used. On 8 November 3,000 copies were ordered; on 2 December 3,000; on 13 December 4,000; on 17 January 3,000; on 24 March 5,000. After these eight impressions, comprising 24,300 copies, had been taken off, the type was too much worn to admit of further use, and the book was reset in the same form and electrotyped. The so-called ninth impression appeared in June 1930, two months after Bridges's death. In August an entirely new edition appeared, a foolscap 4to set in 12-on-15-point Fournier and printed on specially manufactured paper: of this 'second edition' (as it is called on the dust-jacket) Bridges himself, reluctantly impressed by the indignation of many readers at the smallness of the type he had chosen for the 8vo, had approved a specimen page some weeks before he died.

I have outlined only the publishing history of *The Testament of Beauty*. The textual history remains to be written. But it may be opportune to conclude with a note on the significance of the various printings after the private edition and the first impression in 8vo. The second, third, and fourth impressions followed too hard on publication for the author to be able to make alterations: in the second, however, the printer corrected one or two small errors. Bridges's first revisions reached the Press when half the fifth impression had been printed off, with the result that only those in Books III and IV could be made and those in Books I and II were reserved for the sixth impression. These revisions amounted to less than a dozen and were aimed only at consistency of spelling ('politick' and 'relyeth') or at restoring, in 'archæology' and 'Chaldæan', the ligatured diphthong which Hart had many years earlier banished from the style book of the Press. In the seventh impression the printer restored to 'Cæsar' a ligature which had been overlooked. For the eighth Bridges provided a thorough revision. Even here, out of some 170 alterations, the greater number were again points of spelling—among others 'thatt' for 'that' in nineteen places, 'wil' for 'will' in fifteen, the deletion of a final mute 'e' ('wer', 'hav', 'natur', 'disparat') in more than twenty, and a reversion to the original spelling of 'relieth'—or they introduced hyphens or altered punctuation or paragraphing. Verbal changes occur at I. 6, 252, 332, 630–1, 645, and 707; II. 59, 470, 497, and 616–18; III. 204, 594, 650, 699, 801, 862, 865, 880, and 908; IV. 459, 512, 1101, and 1209. The posthumous 'ninth impression' contains one last alteration, in the Aristotelian tag at IV. 71: this is the final text, to be preferred, owing to its greater accuracy, to the Fournier 4to.

Up to the end of 1946 there had been printed at Walton Street 57,370 copies of *The Testament of Beauty*, and in the U.S.A. there had been printed and sold 10,600.

# VI

## PERSONAL NAMES IN TROLLOPE'S POLITICAL NOVELS

*By* R. W. CHAPMAN

γλῶσσαν ἐν τύχᾳ νέμων. AESCHYLUS

IN the minor matters of Trollope's fiction nothing better exhibits his instinct for propriety than his choice of names, personal and local. The *Autobiography* is, I think, silent on this matter; but evidence of his interest will be found in *Can You Forgive Her?*, chapter 16, where in a footnote he acknowledges a debt to Thackeray: 'Had he been left with us he would have forgiven me my little theft.' The stolen name was Lord Cinquebars (i.e. a five-barred gate) for a hunting 'scion of nobility'.

He indulges, indeed, a mode now generally rejected: the significant or punning name. But that fashion has the authority of Aeschylus and Shakespeare. As practised by the Victorians it must be judged on performance. It can sink as low as in Dickens's Lord Frederick Verisopht; it can rise as high as Mr. Wodehouse's Lord Blicester, a joke which the author shares with that privileged minority of his readers who know that Bicester in Oxfordshire is pronounced Bister.

The pun is not, of course, the sole determinant. In naming his major persons Trollope is in general content to follow nature, which has invested many names with social, and even moral, attributes derived in part at least from their forms, not merely from historical association. So his Pallisers and Fitzhowards and Tregears connote nobility or gentility, just as Arnold's Stiggins, Higginbottom, and Wragg suggest their contrary. But nature not seldom achieves a more particular propriety. What fitter names could be found for artists in poetry than Alfred Tennyson and Algernon Swinburne; than Sir Richard Grenville for a gallant die-hard; than Lucius Cary, Viscount Falkland, for a pacific cavalier; than Narcissus Luttrell for a fastidious book-collector? Sometimes nature herself condescends to the felicity of a pun. Invention could not better Sir Bindon Blood, or Aylmer Firebrace, late chief of the London Fire Brigade. I should be tempted to regard the Earl of Donoughmore as a 'natural' for an idle peer, were not the present holder of that title in fact conspicuous for public service.

In his punning invention Trollope excels his rivals. There are, no doubt, banalities; Greenacre and Lookaloft may pass in low comedy, but they are poor fooling. Doctors Filgrave and Rerechild, on the other hand, are so plausible that we forgive, or even forget, the pun. Sir Omicron Pie is an acknowledged masterpiece; I know households in which any eminent consultant is Sir Omicron. That is not strictly a pun; I suppose the Greek letters suggest the cabalistic mysteries of the healing art.

At their best Trollope's puns may even escape detection. I cannot doubt that Matching Priory[1] glances at Lady Glencora's propensities, or at her own forced marriage; but I had long been familiar with the house before this struck me. Even as I write, it occurs that the borough of Tankerville (*vide infra*) must be from *tankard*. If Trollope remembered that Tankerville is also an ancient Northumbrian earldom, he may have pleased himself with the ambiguity. One of my friends is reluctant to believe that Stalham, the seat (in *Ayala's Angel*) of Sir Harry Albury, M.F.H., is 'stall 'em', i.e. Sir Harry's hunters.

It is understood that a complete *Lexicon Trollopianum* will soon be produced by American research. Hitherto there is no guide to these matters except the meritorious 'Who's Who in Barsetshire' appended to one edition of the Barchester novels. Partly for that reason, the present desultory study is based mainly on recollection, and some re-reading, of the 'political' series, in which, moreover, Trollope shows his consummate mastery of this art.

*A Jove principium.* A prince just crosses the stage of *Phineas Redux*, all tact and affability. Otherwise Trollope hardly flies at royalty. But the Victorian political world was so permeated with aristocracy that a political novelist was bound to spend much of his time in the houses of the great, where Trollope was at once and completely at his ease. What could be more ducal than his dukes? I do not defend the pun in Gatherum Castle;[2]

---

[1] Cf. Mistletoe, a ducal seat in *The American Senator*.
[2] Omnium Gatherum, 'Let 'em all come', is recorded in *O.E.D.* from 1530.

but that is taken over from an earlier book; in his later period Trollope's lords and their seats are not very often significant in the technical sense. But by a lucky chance Omnium suits very well the wealth and sublime selfishness of the elder duke, the wealth and arrogant altruism of his nephew and successor. The younger man's other names are an inspiration: Plantagenet Palliser. He was 'Planty Pall' in the clubs; but did any man ever call him either?[1] His wife calls him 'Plantagenet'; perhaps Mr. Bonteen may have called him 'Palliser'. But he did that, or something like it, once too often, and was told that he had 'forgotten himself'. There is also the 'other' or 'old' duke, of St. Bungay, who had served in Liberal ministries for half a century. I must suppose him in some degree modelled on the third Lord Lansdowne, 'the Nestor of the Whigs'. If I am right in this, Trollope has covered his tracks, calling him Fitzhoward and placing him at Long Royston in Norfolk; this suggests a conflation of two East Anglian dukes, Fitzroy Duke of Grafton and Howard Duke of Norfolk. The Lansdowne family is another Fitz, Fitzmaurice; but its roots are in the west country.

Trollope's prime ministers and other political leaders raise various questions. Lords Brock and de Terrier may mean no more than party strife, perhaps with an implication that they would rather be friendly in the country than sparring at Westminster. One might have expected that Brock (badger) would be the Conservative, clinging to office in spite of a hostile majority in the House of Commons, de Terrier his natural foe. But in fact Brock is the Liberal, de Terrier the Conservative premier. It may be an accident that the name Mildmay suggests the even temper and gentle manners of a beloved chief. But Monk, equally non-committal, suits well the character of a self-effacing incorruptible. Turnbull is well chosen for a truculent radical leader, and Bonteen for a vulgar and unscrupulous careerist.

[1] 'Planty Pall, as he is familiarly called.' *Phineas Finn*, chapter 29. If anyone is guilty of this familiarity to his face, I shall be surprised. Trollope may be inconsistent; in *Phineas Finn* Palliser is made to shoot a stag, a feat of which he is later represented as incapable. But the question is answered, I find, in *The Small House at Allington*, chapter 43: 'The duke was the only living being who called him Plantagenet to his face, though there were some scores of men who talked of Planty Pall behind his back.'

When we come to Daubeny and Gresham we are, I think, on surer ground. Trollope in his *Autobiography*, chapter 20, expressly states that his leading politicians are 'more or less portraits, not of living men, but of living political characters'; types, that is, not individuals. I think his memory (which we know, from his confession and otherwise, was treacherous) here deceived him. He must have been aware that Daubeny and Gresham would be taken by his readers to stand for Disraeli and Gladstone, to which they correspond in their initials and in the number of their syllables.[1] Daubeny, moreover, is an elaborate and lifelike portrait of Disraeli as he appeared to Liberals of Trollope's kidney: the audacious, unscrupulous, inscrutable conjurer; the Cagliostro of the age, as he is more than once termed. The case of Gresham is less clear; but his commanding intellect, his abounding eloquence,—perhaps also his arrogant manner and his ungovernable temper?—seem to point to Gladstone.

Chronology may be significant. I offer a list of the novels, with their dates of publication and the political leaders in each:

|  | Liberal | Conservative |
|---|---|---|
| *Can You Forgive Her?* 1864–5 | Brock |  |
| *Phineas Finn,* 1867–9 | Mildmay | de Terrier |
| *The Eustace Diamonds,* 1871–3 | Gresham |  |
| *Phineas Redux,* 1873 | Gresham | Daubeny |
| *Prime Minister,* 1875–6 |  | Daubeny |
| *The Duke's Children,* 1879–80 | Monk | Drummond |

The circumstances of *The Prime Minister* are exceptional: Gresham retires (temporarily), and the Duke of Omnium heads a Coalition government.

Now the relevant dates in the careers of the possible prototypes of some of Trollope's leaders seem to be these: Palmerston (Brock?) died in 1865. Derby (de Terrier?) resigned 1868, died 1869. Disraeli (Daubeny?) became Prime Minister 1868, resigned 1868, became Prime Minister 1874, resigned 1880, died 1881. Gladstone (Gresham?) became Prime Minister 1868, again 1873, resigned the leadership 1875, became Prime

---

[1] In *Phineas Finn,* chapter 3, we are told that Daubeny was commonly shortened to 'Dubby', which suggests 'Dizzy'; but the abbreviation is not, I think, repeated. The syllable *ben* may suggest Benjamin.

Minister again 1880. It will be seen that the coincidences, though not complete, are striking.

I note, further, that in these novels Trollope very rarely names a living politician.[1] It would have been clumsy to mix fact and fiction by doing so. I must, however, concede occasional exceptions to this. In one or two places[2] contemporary politicians are named; but they are named with politicians outside the period, Walpole, or Burke, or Peel; clearly the real and the fictitious could not be combined in such a reference. In *The Eustace Diamonds* (ch. 4) Gladstone and Bright are named. That may be explained, or excused, by the fact that the book is almost non-political. Finally, in *Phineas Finn*, ch. 18, Monk quotes Palmerston as saying 'that it wouldn't do for an English Minister to have his hall door opened by a maid-servant'. This is not unlike some anecdotes of Lord Brock.

These tentative conclusions are confirmed, I think, by the political episodes of *Framley Parsonage*. There, in chapter 8, the Whig Prime Minister who 'had brought the Russian war to a close' and 'had had wonderful luck in that Indian Mutiny', is not named, but is obviously Palmerston, who is named, with Aberdeen and Derby, in chapter 11. Later in the book, chapter 18, when real politics give way to imaginary politics— the Lord Petty Bag and the appointment of a Barchester prebendary—the Whig Prime Minister becomes Lord Brock, and his successful rivals are Lord de Terrier and Sidonia, who are clearly Derby and Disraeli.

In general (Prime Ministers excepted) Trollope is content to let his aristocracy read like an extract from the real Peerage. Brentford, Chiltern, Standish, Effingham, Percival, Soulsby, Harrington are simply good English family or place names. But there are idiosyncrasies. Trollope has a predilection for Scottish names: Earl of Midlothian, Marquis of Auld Reekie, Lady Macleod, Lord Nidderdale, and many more. One wonders why he saddled his Glencora with the impossible surname M'Cluskie. Does it perhaps add a touch to the uncongenial environment that helps us to condone a loveless marriage?

---

[1] In the Barchester books, to which politics are only incidental, Palmerston and other politicians are often named and sometimes discussed, e.g. in *Framley Parsonage*, ch. 8.                                  [2] *Phineas Redux*, chs. 22, 58.

## TROLLOPE'S POLITICAL NOVELS

Even in the ranks of nobility Trollope sometimes allows his names to suggest baseness, and oftener to suggest folly, as in Lord Fawn, an 'innocent', or Lord Popplecourt, a nonentity, or notably Lord Dumbello, whose mouth was better fitted for sucking the knob of his cane than for articulate speech. I suspect an innuendo in Hartletop, the marquisate to which Dumbello succeeded, but cannot fix it. I offer no defence for Lord Earlybird, the assiduous philanthropist (perhaps suggested by the great Lord Shaftesbury?) whose Garter did him no good and the Prime Minister some harm.

When he comes to the middle class Trollope gives a looser rein to his fancy. His squires and parsons are for the most part named with no special or obvious intention. But felicities abound. If the relatively penniless son of a Cornish gentleman must aspire to the hand of a duke's daughter, he gets a flying start by being Francis Oliphant Tregear. Beauty and daring, without principle and without conscience, speak in the name Burgo Fitzgerald. I do not find Burgo in the *Oxford Dictionary of Christian Names*; *ben trovato*? At the other extreme, sterling worth and solid independence are conveyed in many monosyllables, as in Squire Dale of Allington, or John Grey, the bookish country-gentleman and tenacious lover of *Can You Forgive Her?*, who came within the Palliser orbit and had membership of Parliament thrust upon him.

There are many comic characters in this class. There is for instance Mr. Spooner of Spoon Hall. I suppose that if Trollope had been challenged he might have replied that Spooner is a good English name; and this is a good example of the innuendo that can be taken or left at choice. To minor politicians and party hacks Trollope shows no mercy. The Tweedledum and Tweedledee of parliamentary management, Roby and Ratler, recall Disraeli's caricature, in *Coningsby*, of Croker. For a dry stick we have Sir Orlando Drought, for a stuffed shirt Sir Timothy Beeswax, or Sir Marmaduke Morecombe, Chancellor of the Duchy. The silent member for Tankerville, Mr. Browborough, who lost his seat by excess of bribery, is as aptly named as his corrupt constituency. We touch bottom with Mr. Bott, the political jackal who conspired with Mrs. Marsham to spy on 'Lady Glencowrer', and with Quintus Slide, the muckraking editor of 'The People's Banner'.

When he enters the regions of vice or dissipation Trollope is less happy. The names, if not merely neutral, are too often merely sordid without other aptitude. A fair specimen is the Roebury Club in *Can You Forgive Her?* Its hunting, card-playing, drinking members are 'Maxwell the banker', 'Grindley the would-be fast attorney' (usually 'Grindems'), Calder Jones, M.P., Pollock 'a sporting literary gentleman', and George Vavasor, the villain of the book. I prefer the company of the Beargarden Club; not the den of iniquity that figures in *The Way We Live Now*, but the much milder establishment of *The Duke's Children*. Members are Silverbridge (the Duke's heir), Adolphus Longstaff, 'whom men within the walls of this asylum sometimes call Dolly', Lord Nidderdale, and the inimitable 'Major' Tifto, Master of the Runnymede Hounds. The five letters are crammed with hints: the 'Major' was among other things a tuft-hunter and a racing tipster or tout. Similar sportsmen are the undesirables whom the blundering Duchess entertained at Gatherum, Captain Gunner and Major Pountney. The latter I take to be phonetically Puntny (he is addressed as 'Punt') and to suggest *punter*. A more lovable character is Major Caneback in *The American Senator*, who feared neither man nor 'Bonebreaker' and met death accordingly.

I recall no very interesting legal names except that of Chaffanbrass the ruthless barrister, whose defence of Phineas is the culminating triumph in the grand panorama of *Phineas Redux*. I am puzzled by Lord Moles, who is just mentioned as 'the expiring Lord Chancellor' in *Phineas Finn* (ch. 8). Since he appears, I believe, once only, his name is almost certainly significant (see below). But of what? Can it be dissyllabic, in allusion to Virgil's *tantae molis*? Or does it glance at the historical Lord Chancellor Cairns?

It is a novelist's plain duty to make his names probable, as well as possible, in relation to his persons' origin and environment. He may not call a Yorkshireman Angus Macdonald, or a great landowner Lord Jones, or a grocer Montmorency. But when it comes to fitting a name to a nature, thought is free. There is no reason in the facts of life why a heroine should not be Jane Smith and her maid Shirley Keeldar. Strictly, indeed, it is by poetic licence that beautiful names are given to beautiful women, and plain names to homely folks. But we all feel that a novelist must avail himself of this licence, though it entails some sacrifice of accuracy. As Jane Austen remarks[1] of the union of pathos and corpulence, 'there are unbecoming conjunctions which taste cannot tolerate'. It is here, therefore, that an author's invention is most severely tested.

Phineas Finn, of all Trollope's young men perhaps the most engaging, to us as to all the clever men and women who found him irresistible, is not named with any special felicity. Phineas is merely odd, Finn merely Irish? But his friends, in the House and in the hunting-field, and the women who fell in love with him or just escaped it, make a brave nominal roll. There is Barrington Erle, who will never be more than an Under-Secretary, and Larry Fitzgibbon, who never did a day's work in his parliamentary career; and Chiltern, who made Phineas fight a foolish duel and became his friend for life. And the women; we are apt to forget Mary Flood Jones, the first Mrs. Finn, whom Trollope had to kill because she interfered with Phineas's 'come-back'; we do not forget Laura Standish, nor Violet Effingham, nor the second Mrs. Finn, who before her second marriage was Marie Goesler, better known as Madame Max. Her origin was and is obscure; it is not clear whether she was a Jewess by birth or merely a Jew banker's widow. But she is the rarest of Trollope's many exotics, and is as finely and exotically named. Chiltern, Phineas's rival, friend, and foil, is his father's heir and is therefore hardly allowed to have a Christian name. But his sister and his wife sometimes call him Oswald. Oswald Standish suits well a red-headed fire-eater, saved from vice and idleness by a tactful wife and the autocracy of the Brake Hunt.

In naming places Trollope has the same *curiosa felicitas* as in naming their inmates. Most of his towns, villages, and houses have ordinary names, like Barchester, or Loughton, or Framley Court, or Plumstead Episcopi. But the comic spirit is always at hand to seize an opportunity. I have mentioned Matching, and Stalham, and Spoon Hall. There are even bolder flights. Killancodlem, Mrs. Montacute Jones's Highland palace, is an atrocious pun. But it is not more cacophonously absurd than Killiecrankie; perhaps it is that resemblance that saves it.

[1] *Persuasion* (ch. 8).

Even Crummie Toddie, the neighbouring shooting-lodge, is plausible enough. More serious implications are not very common. But there is romance, heightened by irony, in Lough[1] Linter, the scene first of Laura Standish's fatal mistake, later of her husband's descent into parsimony and madness. I find a northern, moorland bleakness in the dilapidations of Grex; and though, as I have said, Monk may be a neutral name, there is no missing the sinister intention of Sir Cosmo Monk of Monkshade, whose wicked wife plotted with Burgo to undermine Glencora's virtue.

Most of Trollope's worst, that is, his most blatantly obvious, names have this excuse, that they are given to very minor persons, who must be labelled but need not be particularized. Thus of Mr. Finespun we need know no more than that he was a doctrinaire financier and a difficult colleague; of Messrs. Foolscap, Margin, and Vellum no more than that they were attorneys of repute. I am afraid that 'young Lord Cantrip from the Colonies', that is, from the Colonial Office (*Phineas Finn*, ch. 29) is 'can-trip', with reference to globe-trotting. Lord and Lady Cantrip are not very minor persons; they become conspicuous enough in the sequel. But perhaps the Colonial Secretary was on his first introduction expected to make only a passing appearance. Even this unhappy *paronomasia* has the excuse that it is natural to divide it (as I long did) 'cant-rip' and so reduce it to harmless non-significance.

Trollope's preoccupation with names chimes with the working of his creative imagination, which he tells us began from persons, not from theme or action. He had, he declares, no talent for plots; the incidents that revealed his characters were devised as he wrote. But he had by then long lived with his people, getting to know them, watching them grow up and change, following them, sometimes, into old age and the grave. It was doubtless, to him, of paramount and exceptional importance that they should have proper names.

*Note.*—The learned editor of *The Trollopian* directs me to Trollope's letter of 31 March 1869 to the *Daily Telegraph*, which on that day had printed an article accusing him of 'having drawn portraits of the leading politicians of the time', and especially of drawing a

[1] It should be *Loch*. I suppose Trollope's familiarity with Ireland led him astray.

malicious portrait of John Bright as Mr. Turnbull. 'I depicted Mr. Bright neither in his private or public character; and I cannot imagine how any likeness justifying such a charge against me can be found.' The letter contains also a general disclaimer; but this is not emphasized, and it is significant that Trollope makes no reference to the *Telegraph*'s other identifications, viz.

    de Terrier = Derby     Mildmay = Russell
    Daubeny = Disraeli    Gresham = Gladstone

# VII
## THE DIFFUSION OF IDEAS
### By R. C. K. ENSOR

I

SUPPOSE that to-day in the middle of the twentieth century an idea or a doctrine comes to birth, what are the various channels by which it may be diffused to the minds of men? Eight will probably occur to everyone as pre-eminent—newspapers, radio, and films; periodicals, books, and plays; universities and schools. Of these the first three reach all classes, thinking and unthinking alike; the second three preponderantly affect the thinking class; while the last two are in a category somewhat aside, the universities playing a great part in the origination of ideas, while the part of the schools is limited in the main to diffusing what has been originated elsewhere.

Suppose that we next move a hundred years backward, and ask what were the corresponding channels of publicity in the middle of the nineteenth century. Again we may count eight of them, but they will not be the same eight. The first three will be newspapers, sermons, and public meetings. The other five will be as above, unless indeed we leave out plays; the British stage of, say, 1847 having sunk to a level at which its contribution to the nation's mental processes was of small importance. No equivalents for radio or films existed.

Move back yet another hundred years, to the middle of the eighteenth century; and the picture is different again. Newspapers were then in their infancy. Pamphlets and broadsheets, and occasionally periodicals, appeared on a small scale. The chief products of the printing-press were books. The few licensed theatres drew packed audiences, and the leading actor of the day was Garrick; but, apart from making Shakespeare better known, the stage could not compare with the book as a vehicle of ideas. The sermon had importance, though less than in the mid-seventeenth century, and less again than in the mid-nineteenth.

A brief comparative glance like the foregoing might be developed in detail in all sorts of directions. Take for instance the channels by which a public opinion has been formed about books. To-day this is done systematically by book reviews, as already had been the case a century earlier. But in the eighteenth century it was not so. Books were then largely published by subscription; the publisher or the author, or both, canvassed members of the very limited class which could afford them, and thus aimed to cover the expense in advance. To achieve this, and also to promote further sales among this limited class, the helpful thing was to get commendations from some of the leaders of Church or State or Society—the elegant Lord X, patron of literature, or the learned divine, Bishop Y. The fate of books was not decided by reviewers. Some of the earliest references to them in connexion with new books occur in Cowper's letters (from 1782); but Cowper could afford to regard them with indifference, almost with contempt. What later compelled authors to take them more seriously was the advent of the great nineteenth-century 'Reviews', headed by the *Edinburgh* (1802) and the *Quarterly* (1807). It was in 1819 that the *Quarterly Review* published the article which was widely supposed to have killed Keats. It makes no difference for our purpose that he in fact died from other causes; what is relevant is that so many of his friends (including Shelley) believed that a review could kill an author—a notion hardly conceivable in Cowper's day.

The foundation of the *Athenaeum* (1828) made the new kind of reviewing a weekly affair, and led to an increase in the proportion of new books reviewed. But it was only towards the very end of the nineteenth century that book reviews came to the fore in daily newspapers. H. W. Massingham's literary editorship of the *Daily Chronicle* made something of an epoch in that respect; while *The Times* contrived for some years to keep the unwelcome novelty out of its columns by relegating it to the separate *Times Literary Supplement*, founded for that purpose in 1902. Much later, indeed mainly after 1919, came the development of book-reviewing in two great Sunday newspapers; which carried critiques of the quality associated with the 'highbrow' weeklies to vastly larger publics than the weeklies have ever reached.

Take, again, the case of sermons. Sermons in England have never come quite to the top as a form of literature. We have had no golden age of pulpit eloquence like that which in France comprises the great names of Bossuet, Bourdaloue, Fénelon, and Massillon. But for three centuries and a half, from Latimer down to Liddon and Spurgeon, the sermon was a leading influence in English life. It is so no longer: primarily owing to the decline in church attendance; but partly, in the Established Church, to the revulsion from a Protestant outlook centred on the pulpit to a sacramental one centred on the altar; and partly, of course, to the competition of other interests. The clergy's chief remedy, as they felt their hold on audiences slackening, was to shorten their discourses—a policy which by degrees has brought them to the ten-minute 'sermonette' of to-day, i.e. to a length within which only a very exceptional man indeed can convey anything of real moment to his hearers.

Or take the case of public meetings. Speeches at them differ from sermons, not merely because they are secular, but because the hearers have freedom to heckle the speaker, a fact which profoundly alters the relation between him and them. Between 1832 and 1914 meetings filled, probably, a much greater space in people's lives than they do now. They are still held on the occasion of parliamentary elections and of some (though by no means all) local ones; but even then the average attendance is not what it used to be. Here, as with the sermon, one must allow for the counter-attraction of rival interests; and, having regard to the date when the falling-off occurred, there seems little doubt what the main counter-attraction has been. It has been that of the cinema. The change does not concern towns only; it affects the country-side as much or more. In the nineteenth century English villagers had few evening recreations; a 'penny reading', a magic lantern, a concert, a high tea—these were rare godsends. Between them public meetings, whether political, religious, local, or to push some cause like a friendly society or a co-operative store, drew audiences automatically. But to-day the villager, thanks to country bus services, can visit the nearest town cinemas several times a week; and with a local dance-hall sometimes also available he can satiate his appetite for evening diversion without going to hear speeches.

## THE DIFFUSION OF IDEAS

Many people accustomed to associate British liberty with the right of all and sundry to hold public meetings may be surprised at the suggestion that the platform has lost its importance. Yet nobody whose public memory goes back fifty years can doubt it—at least for the time being. What is in question is not the right but the practice. Of course the vogue for meetings always fluctuated with the political interests of a given time; but the present is a case of more than fluctuation. The last great boom in meetings occurred during the rise of the Labour Party, when Socialism came as a new evangel, which people paid to hear orally from the eloquent lips of Keir Hardie or Philip Snowden. Labour meetings are still held, but they are not like that; and the party now, like other parties, relies mainly for the diffusion of its ideas upon various forms of the printed word. If there has been any come-back for oral eloquence, it is on the radio; but there the audience are even less able to interrupt the speaker than in church.

Newspapers, radio, and films alike are to-day nation-wide, as no medium save the sermon ever was before. A century ago 10,000 was a large circulation for a morning daily. To-day five of them taken together sell about ten million copies; and that does not include any of the 'quality' newspapers, one of which has recently attained the million scale. In the towns nearly every house takes a morning newspaper, and a large proportion buy an evening one besides. On Sunday there is an orgy of newspaper-reading, especially in working-class homes; where one 'low-brow' journal has all the dailies beaten handsomely. The radio is equally universal; over ten million households in Great Britain pay the licence for a receiving set. The films are in a different case; of the more highly educated people a proportion go to them only occasionally. But for probably at least eighty per cent. of the adult community their vogue is enormous; and it goes along with a force of impact corresponding to what Horace said 2,000 years earlier about the superiority of optical over aural impressions.

There are of course other channels, the most important being posters. But the poster is almost solely of advertising importance; it only occasionally diffuses a non-commercial idea. Science and invention, however, which gave us the films and radio, cannot be limited to them. A third claimant already knocks at the door—television. It is in truth a sort of hybrid between the last two, and destined, in the view of its more ardent sponsors, to make great inroads on both of them. As yet it remains relatively costly, but the goal of its mass-development seems not far off.

## II

Now let us consider some more general effects of these differences in the channels which diffuse ideas. Comparing in particular the mid-nineteenth century with the mid-twentieth, are the changes, on balance, improvements? Mechanically and in the sphere of human contrivance they unquestionably are. But to-day much bitter experience has taught us, what a hundred years ago men had not learned, that advances in science and invention often subtract from human happiness more than they add to it.

The first feature, which few people can fail to notice, in to-day's channels of publicity is the immensely increased force which they bring to bear on the individual. This is partly due to their affecting simultaneously far larger proportions of the population; for any impression received by an individual is much magnified, if he is conscious that a crowd also receives it. Newspapers and the radio, as we have noted, reach nearly everybody. Schooling, too, has long been universal, at least in its primary phases (though it was not a century ago); and now the Butler Act has—on paper, at all events—made secondary education universal as well.

Higher education in the full sense can never be for everybody; still less can the effective intramural membership of universities. But the percentage of the nation's youth admitted to these higher developments in one form or another has been multiplied many times. It now includes both sexes, as a century ago it did not; and in other respects it represents a much wider influence up and down the country. At the same time it has changed its character. Higher education a century ago was limited to a few subjects; but those were mainly cultural, and the result was a cultivated and critical mind. To-day the subjects are legion; but the tendency to specialize early on a single (often non-cultural) one causes many recipients of higher education to be little better at forming sane opinions (little less apt, that is, to seesaw between credulity and suspicion) than the uneducated. Thus the multiplication of men and women who have passed higher examinations has not multiplied thinking people in the same proportion; although it has multiplied them.

Yet universal education is crucial, not only in itself, but because it opens doors to so much else. Even for following the films or the radio capacity to read helps; but for the newspaper it is indispensable. The newspaper (and not the book) may indeed be regarded as the principal beneficiary of the Education Acts. The weight of its impact on the public is now far greater than a century ago. Not that a *Times* leading article of 1947 has more influence on government than a *Times* leading article of 1847; perhaps it usually has less. But the Press's power of suggestion, its capacity to create an 'atmosphere', has grown enormously. In political matters it is modified and mitigated—in Britain, at all events—by the still wide variety of ownerships and the variety of schools of thought which they represent. To get a fuller idea of it, one must go outside political controversy and study the feats of commercial advertising. Here is a random example of what it can do.

Between the two World Wars there was in England a remarkable development, under enterprising leadership, of the industry growing fruit (chiefly tomatoes, melons, and cucumbers) under glass. The difficulty in this industry had always been to synchronize demand with supply. Fruits are perishable, and at the periods of peak output there had been enormous wastages. To overcome them the slogan 'Eat more fruit' was invented. Through its use not only was the public induced to consume far more glasshouse fruits, but by a skilful timing and graduation of the advertising campaign the ups and downs of demand were made to follow the ups and downs of supply with such nicety that wastages were ironed out. The interest to us here of this particular anti-glut technique lies in what it exemplifies —viz. the effective though unobtrusive control which newspapers can exert by suggestion over the tastes and acts of their public. No control matching that in degree was wielded by any medium of publicity a hundred years ago, unless conceivably by the sermon.

The second feature that will strike us about the channels of publicity to-day in contrast to those of Queen Victoria's day (and still more, of course, to those of George II's) is the immensely wider reception which they procure for a single transmission, or, to vary the metaphor, their mass-production quality. One sees this most with the newest of them. Thus the prime characteristic of the film, the grand difference between it and the play, is that whereas a play to be shown in five theatres at once must have five different casts of actors to perform it, a film may be shown in hundreds of cinemas at once, but every showing is of the same single performance. Similarly in the case of the radio. If a statesman wishes to address the nation by way of public meetings, he will have to travel the country, confront many separate audiences, and deliver as many separate speeches; yet even so most of his countrymen will not hear his words, but only read them or read about them. Whereas if he employs the radio he need merely utter into the microphone a single speech, and it then, with the living tones and inflections of his own voice, can be heard all over Britain by anyone who switches on one of its ten or eleven million receiving-sets. Moreover, if recorded, it can be repeated over and over again at different hours for listeners whom the original hour did not suit.

Nor is the case very different with modern newspapers. The modern popular journal, which goes to two or three million purchasers every morning, is essentially a triumph of large-scale economy. The proportion of consumers to producers has risen exceptionally in this field; one voice, or at least one chorus, speaks to those millions of ears. By contrast the book, it may be said, does not exemplify the tendency in any similar degree. Yet even in book production remarkable economies can be realized by producing on a very large scale; and that was the basis of the very cheap reprints so prominent in the thirties, before the war and paper-rationing constricted the book industry. Although the tendency had as yet not gone far in relation to new books, there seemed no reason why it eventually should not—with results adverse to new authors.

The third feature that claims our attention arises out of the other two. It is the growing temptation to the State to control the channels of publicity. One of the tyrants of antiquity is said to have wished that the people had a single neck. It would

## THE DIFFUSION OF IDEAS 89

render decapitation so much easier. The concentrations, which have just been noticed, have that effect; a single broadcasting system, or a single film shown at multitudinous cinemas, or a small number of popular newspapers each circulating in millions, are plainly easier for the State to discipline than were, say, some thousands of preachers scattered all over the country each fulminating from his own separate pulpit. At the same time the far greater influence, which these concentrated powers can exert over public life, creates at once a challenge and a lure for State interference.

In order to see how far this may go, we must look outside Great Britain. The facts just noted, most of which can be paralleled in some degree in any contemporary country, form the starting-point of what is now called the Totalitarian State. The great discovery of Lenin—indeed, it may be thought, his only discovery—was that by not merely controlling but converting into engines of government all the immensely powerful agencies which are available in a modern society for creating and diffusing ideas—the newspaper and the book, the film and the stage-play, the radio and the platform, the school and the university, not to mention the poster and the picture and even, so far as is practicable, the pulpit—it is possible to build up despotism on an entirely new footing, far more solid than any on which it had ever rested before. The old despotisms relied almost entirely on physical force, exerted through police and soldiers. The new despotisms do not cease to employ it, but they cease to regard it as basic; the basis of their rule is mental force. The distinction, of course, is not absolute. Hume said long ago that the most despotic governments are founded upon opinion, if only upon the opinion of the despot's bodyguard. Thus in 1917 what made possible the fall of the Russian Tsarism was the mutiny of the Imperial Guards, typified by the famous Preobrazhensky Regiment. Awareness of this danger had led despotisms of the older type to set up censorships for newspapers, books, plays, and such other channels of publicity as from time to time might seem important. But their action in the mental sphere was rather negative than positive. Characteristic was their policy regarding illiteracy, which they were seldom eager to remove, since it saved the masses from reading subversive literature. The new kind of despotism does exactly the opposite:

it strives to get rid of illiteracy as fast as it can, so that all its subjects may soak their minds in the pro-Government publications, which are all that the State allows to reach them. It may like to ascribe this policy to an idealist passion for education; but in fact it is a perfectly logical part of the neo-despotic technique.

At the same time, just because it opens the eyes and ears of its people, the new system has to be far more careful than earlier despotism was that they shall not see or hear anything inspiring 'dangerous thoughts'. Its censorship is much more complete. Under the French autocracy in the eighteenth century writers like Rousseau and Voltaire got home, despite censorship, to the hearts and minds of Frenchmen; and under the nineteenth-century Tsarism a similar state of things existed for Russians in regard to writers like Tolstoy and Turgeniev and Herzen and so many others. Moreover if an author felt stifled at home, he could go into foreign exile, and do his writing there. None of these possibilities exist in a Totalitarian State. The State is the only publisher; no citizen is allowed to go out of the country except on State service; and no foreign-published books, except such classics as may be deemed innocuous, can come in. An impenetrable 'iron curtain' around the national territory ensures that the state-controlled channels of publicity shall have an entire monopoly of the diffusion of ideas within it.

This way of conducting the despotic government of a country is something entirely new. In earlier centuries the conditions did not exist which, as we have seen, render it possible. So far it has everywhere been from the standpoint of those running it an unqualified success. Hitler's State and Mussolini's perished alike through external war; but in no single instance has a Totalitarian State been overthrown from within. Nor is it easy to see how one could be, when once firmly established; for even a conflict of personalities at the highest level can only be conceived as changing the despots, not the despotism.

The difference between Totalitarian theory and nearly all nineteenth-century political thinking might be described in Kant's famous phrase as 'Copernican'. The nineteenth century sought ways of securing that government should conform to public opinion. Public opinion was conceived as being, in the last resort, something above control—a natural force, a free wind that ought to blow where it listed; and government as something more flexible and malleable, that as far as possible should be accommodated to it. Conversely the Totalitarian view aims, not at conforming government to public opinion, but at conforming public opinion to government. Government is conceived as a predetermined group of men despotically pursuing predetermined policies. The malleable thing is public opinion, which by suitable hammering can be so shaped as not merely to accept those men and those policies, but to give them active and even fanatical support through thick and thin.

### III

How far are we in Great Britain removed from any development of this kind? It is easy to rule it out *a priori* by reference to the country's long tradition of liberty and the mental habits of her people. But is that really warranted? The common people of this island to-day, crowded in great cities, herded in great industries, and taking orders from great trade unions, over all of which they have as individuals very little control, undergo environmental influences quite different from those which in the past shaped the individualist John Bull. When one adds to that the effect (growing in each case) of standardized houses and clothing, standardized reading and films, standardized sports and recreations, one might naturally expect any party reflecting the common people's temper and outlook to be (as arguably the Labour Party is) more interested in equality than in liberty, and easily led to sacrifice the latter for the former. When, further, one looks beyond the mass-average of the population to the more intellectual and educated types, who provide the expert element in business and public affairs, one is bound to note that those factors in higher education, which from the age of Queen Elizabeth down to that of Queen Victoria specially fostered the ideas of liberty in Great Britain—viz. the Greek and Roman classics and the Bible—are precisely those which to-day the curricula of most students either exclude or do not effectively include. It is scarcely possible to overrate the debt which British liberty has owed during four centuries to the libertarian aspirations of Greece and Rome, with which formerly every boy at a grammar school (to go no farther) was made familiar.

A greater safeguard, perhaps, arises from the fact that the Power which to-day stands out before all others as practising and preaching Totalitarian politics is a Power which ever since the war has taken up an attitude of extreme hostility to Great Britain. If the Totalitarian State were our ally, it may be said, we should run more risk of assimilating its habits than when it is our adversary. There is a good deal in that; and yet it is also true that opponents, as such, are often led to copy one another. The fighting advantages (illustrated in the German and Italian cases as well as in the Russian), which a Totalitarian State derives not only in the national but in the international sphere from its complete simultaneous control of all the channels of publicity, create a standing temptation to the democracies to indulge in counter-measures of a similar control. Should they yield to it, appetite would probably grow with eating.

But these are generalizations. Let us look more closely at some particulars. The only one of the eight main channels of publicity, which in Britain has already passed into direct State ownership, is the radio. It is a very interesting case. The State by Act of Parliament has constituted for itself a monopoly of broadcasting on British soil. From everyone who has a receiving-set within the kingdom it collects a licence-fee; and a fixed proportion of the sum of these fees is paid over to the British Broadcasting Corporation, to which the State has assigned the task of providing a public radio service on the basis of its monopoly. The B.B.C.'s governor and director are appointed by the Government of the day; and there might seem to be here all the ingredients for a State tyranny. But in fact the Corporation, although questions are asked and answered about it in Parliament, enjoys a considerable measure of independence versus the Government. Ministers have, it is true, the right to make personally from time to time announcements or explanatory statements on the air, in order to supply public guidance. Changes in food rationing, in pensions or insurance schemes, in road regulations, or in Budget taxation are all conveniently dealt with in this way, and even (especially during a war) some matters of much broader policy. But the privilege thus granted to Ministers is not supposed to be used for party or personal advantage. Party talks are arranged otherwise—on a rationed

## THE DIFFUSION OF IDEAS

basis, whereby Government and Opposition alike are allotted small quotas of broadcasting time. For the rest, the B.B.C.'s own service aims to be impartial—not in the sense of complete colourlessness, but rather in that prominence given to the views and interests of one side is balanced by equal prominence given to those of the other. Nothing in the world is perfect, but a considerable measure of success here seems to be attested by the fact that the zealots of both parties each habitually charge the B.B.C. staff with favouring the other.

Now how is the B.B.C. kept up to this standard of impartiality and independence? The ultimate safeguards, of course, must be sought in Parliament, where also lie the ultimate dangers. But the day-by-day watchdog is the Press. Many features of the British Press are disputed, but two hardly can be: (1) it is highly competitive; (2) it is very free from subservience to the State, and very critical of such subservience in others. Add that its critical edge, where broadcasting is concerned, is sharpened by some degree of professional jealousy. The result of it all is that we have developed a broadcasting system, in which the material gains of a public monopoly—economies of transmission and of performance, large and equitably raised revenues, freedom from advertisements, planned allocations of time to public interests (e.g. schools broadcasts)—are secured without incurring its most serious disadvantages. But this has been essentially due to the coexistence alongside the nationalized non-competitive radio of a competitive and non-nationalized Press; and without that it seems improbable that it could continue. Some risks are already visible; e.g. that Ministers should use their right of broadcasting too freely and with too partisan a tendency.

The other channels of publicity where the State's control encroaches on those of individuals are the educational—chiefly the schools, but in some measure also the universities. The process belongs mainly to the present century, and is associated with a much-needed multiplication and co-ordination of school facilities. Down to 1890 the State had concerned itself with little but primary education, and 'voluntary' schools loomed large even there. Goschen's grant to the county councils in that year, the report of the Bryce Commission in 1895, the formation of the Board of Education in 1899, and the great Balfour

Education Act in 1902 were the first milestones on the new course. It is not necessary here to list the subsequent developments. They have brought us to a point at which the Government through its Ministry of Education exerts (though in widely varying degrees) a certain control over every school in the country. Even the old-style public schools, so long complete embodiments of educational autonomy, are now subject to State inspection, which some of them much earlier had voluntarily accepted.

The laws and policies applied in this sphere since 1902, culminating in the Butler Education Act, have had three marked results which concern us here: (1) they have increased the control of local education authorities over schools; (2) they have increased the control of the State over local education authorities; (3) they have diminished the control of parents over schools. All three tendencies, it may be thought, were practically and administratively inevitable at an earlier stage in dealing with the kind of education which assures minima. What justifies alarm is their extension to the kind of education whose business is maxima. All three were much enhanced by the Butler Act. By depriving parents of the power to send their children to a secondary school at choice, it deprived the schools of a main motive for considering parents. By greatly reducing the number of local education authorities and confining them outside the great towns to the county councils (i.e. the most bureaucratic of local bodies), it correspondingly fortified Whitehall, and enabled it to set about squeezing education everywhere into a smaller number of prescribed moulds. Thus a machine has been shaped, which any coming régime of a Totalitarian tendency would find exactly fitted to its hand. Is it not most important now to guard against overdoing its operation? Should not our counter-aim everywhere be to retain against it for the organs of higher education (the universities and the higher-grade secondary and technical schools) as much living autonomy as possible? It is probably not an exaggeration to describe this as one of the three or four most fateful current issues in contemporary English life.

Before we leave our subject let us glance at it from yet another angle. Which of all the channels of publicity most subserves freedom? The answer, it is suggested, cannot really be in doubt. It is the book. In contrast with other mediums in which team-work is essential, the book is pre-eminently the organ of individual man speaking to individual men. Compared with film or newspaper or radio or even stage-play, it is almost absurdly easy to produce. And yet its effect is far more concentrated. It takes, for example, a daily drip continued over years before newspapers can get a sure hold over readers. But a single volume once read may change—indeed often has changed—the whole life of its reader. So too the book's small bulk screens it both in place and time. Books alone will penetrate, if anything smuggled can, behind an 'iron curtain'. And a book neglected to-day may yet survive somewhere, until circumstances or the reader arrive which give it its full significance. True, the book needs for its apprehension a greater skill in reading than the newspaper; but improved literacy is one of the few certain improvements in nearly all countries to-day, including especially, as we have seen, the Totalitarian. No lover of liberty therefore should be indifferent to the evolution of the book trade.

Perhaps the most important thing here is that it should remain possible for small and adventurous publishing firms to exist, and for new ones to be born. It would be a bad thing if it ever became as costly and difficult to start a new publishing firm as it now is to start a new morning newspaper. Nevertheless in the book trade as in other trades there are advantages in large-scale business which cannot be gainsaid; and when abnormalities like paper rationing disappear, an increasing proportion of books, and especially of important books, will probably tend to be concentrated in a few firms. This may raise in regard to those firms more sharply than hitherto the question of motive. Are their purposes purely commercial—the making of profit on books exactly as it might be made on calicoes or motor-cars—or do they allow for any higher considerations? It is at this point that the university presses may come to be invested with a peculiar importance. Those, of course, of Oxford and Cambridge have an old renown; but it is fortunate that they have latterly shown themselves capable of so much business development, and also that some of the newer universities are building up presses besides them. Primarily, no doubt, they all exist for educational purposes—

both to ensure the output of text-books which multitudes may want and to finance that of important works which are too learned to sell to a large public. But already they also meet broader and more national needs. So long as the universities themselves retain freedom, that service should increase and not diminish. But on university freedom it all hangs—as indeed what else does not? So far Parliament in Great Britain has been exceptionally wise and self-restrained in its dealings with the universities; one might point to the University Grants Committee as an almost ideal device for contriving that the State should help them without controlling them. But it would be idle to pretend that a good deal of public opinion has not developed in a contrary sense and may not develop further.

# VIII
# THE CHURCH IN THE NINETEENTH CENTURY
## By R. H. MALDEN

CHRONOLOGICALLY the nineteenth century extends from the beginning of the year 1801 to the end of the year 1900. Regarded as an historical epoch it may be held to have begun in 1816, when the end of the long duel with France had secured our supremacy as a world power, and to have lasted until 1914, when the first struggle with Germany shook it.

I believe that that epoch will be recognized as one of the great flowering periods of our race, as were the eighth, thirteenth, and sixteenth centuries.

Our position in 1816 was unassailable. Our command of the sea, which no one could challenge, placed the natural resources of the globe at our disposal. No State has been so predominant since the fall of the Roman Empire, and none has ever abused its power less.

Our economic power kept pace with our political; if indeed it did not outstrip it. Economically events combined in our favour as never before, and as it is unlikely that they ever will again. The greater part of the nineteenth century was the hey-day of the coal-fired steam-engine. That engine was our invention, and we led the way in all its subsequent developments. We had unlimited supplies of the best steam coal in the world. The manufacturing power, which had helped us to fight Napoleon to a standstill, expanded enormously. This, and the almost incredible wealth which it brought, is one of the two factors which have enabled us to save the world from Germany twice. The other is the existence of the British Empire, which reached its final extension with the overthrow of the corrupt and tyrannical governments of the two Boer republics in 1902. It is the fashion now in some circles to speak harshly of 'British Imperialism'. If it is unnecessary to pretend that our record is blameless, it is impossible to deny that unless we had had vast resources outside our own shores we could hardly have stood in 1914, and should certainly have fallen in 1940. Then the German dream would have come true. The world owes to the British Empire the fact that it did not.

Besides our other economic advantages there was during the nineteenth century ample room for our surplus population in North America, whether under our own flag or not, Australia, South Africa, and New Zealand.

It sometimes happens that a great national deliverance from a foreign foe is followed by a remarkable outburst of artistic and intellectual activity. Greece in the fifth century before our era is one instance. Nineteenth-century England is another.

In literature (poetry and prose alike) and painting the roll of famous names is a long one. If music, architecture, and sculpture lagged behind their sisters some creditable work was done in each. Great strides were taken in every branch of natural science: especially, perhaps, in medicine. In the political field there were giants in those days, and real oratory, such as is unknown to us, was to be heard in both Houses of Parliament. Any one who feels disposed to doubt the stature of the leading Victorians, in any walk of life, would do well to spend some hours in the National Portrait Gallery studying their faces.

Social advance was hardly less remarkable. Sir Robert Peel's new Police brought a new security of life and property and soon outlived the suspicion and hostility with which they seem to have been regarded at the outset. As the Executive became more efficient, the Law became more humane. The number of capital offences was reduced from more than a hundred to three: murder, high treason, and arson in the Royal Dockyards. I do not know whether the third of these has outlived wooden ships and the immense stores of inflammable material which they made necessary. Public executions were abolished.

Prisons, the condition of which had been unspeakable, were improved so much that Dickens[1] was inclined to fear that they had become too comfortable. Transportation (for which there was something to be said as long as it was kept within bounds and restricted to young offenders who would be likely to benefit from a fresh start in new surroundings) and imprisonment for debt were abolished.

[1] In *David Copperfield*.

## THE CHURCH IN THE NINETEENTH CENTURY 99

There was also a great revival of interest in education. The Universities of Oxford and Cambridge and the colleges within them underwent various reforms, as did the old public schools. The creation of new universities began with Durham in 1832, and London in 1836, and proceeded apace. A number of new public schools came into being, of which Marlborough has, perhaps, become the most distinguished.

At the beginning of the period the only schools accessible to the children of the poor were those which were provided by the various religious bodies, the Church of England being responsible for some nineteen-twentieths of them. The State began[1] by making a very modest grant[2] towards their maintenance provided that they reached a reasonable standard of efficiency. In 1870 the State began to provide its own schools in districts which voluntary effort had been unable to occupy: which meant the poorer quarters of the large towns. Subsequently a Liberal government made elementary education compulsory, and a Conservative one free. The second of these measures may have been considered to have been made inevitable by the first. Unfortunately the promoters of both did not understand that the life-blood of any system of education is the attitude of public opinion towards it; especially the opinion of the parents of the children concerned. To make it compulsory and free is bound to destroy almost all interest in it, and no expenditure or equipment can make that loss good. But if the fruits of some seventy years of elementary education have proved disappointing, that does not detract from the genuine idealism of the pioneers. It only shows that they had not reckoned sufficiently with the real facts of human nature.

There is, of course, a dark side to all this majestic and enduring achievement. The transformation of England from a thinly populated, mainly agricultural country to a densely populated, mainly manufacturing one meant that the country-side was drained to feed the factories in the large towns, where the overcrowding and squalor became indescribable. The balance between town and country, which we seem to have achieved almost to perfection during the eighteenth century, upon which a healthy national life is now seen to depend, was upset. A number of social problems, which still await solution, were

[1] In 1833.  [2] £20,000 per annum.

created. Amongst other things, the importation of cheap corn and meat from abroad to feed the towns brought England's agriculture (once the equal of any in the world) to the verge of ruin. It has taken the hard experience of two struggles for existence in the present century to teach us that agriculture is at least as important as any other industry, and must not be sacrificed to any other interest.

Throughout the whole period the dominant factor is the increase in the population. At the census taken in 1811 the population of England and Wales was returned at a little over 10 millions. In Gregory King's 'Tables', which appeared in 1688, it is estimated at $5\frac{1}{2}$ millions. He based his calculations on the Hearth Tax, and while his result is not more than a guess, it may be regarded as a shrewd guess. In a hundred and twenty years from his time the population did not quite double itself. But by 1871 the 10 millions had become nearly 23, and by 1911 the 23 millions had become 36. Such a rate of increase was unprecedented, and the difficulties to which it was bound to give rise were aggravated by the fact that it was not distributed evenly throughout the country. The growth of the large towns was still more rapid. Leeds, for instance, increased sevenfold: from about 60,000 to 450,000, and the expansion of Sheffield during the same period was about the same. The record of every large town is similar. Nothing has been affected more deeply and more adversely than the Church by this unforeseen and irresistible development. The basis of the Church is the territorial parish. Almost all parishes were for centuries small and rural, as many still are. If a parish covered a large amount of ground, as was not uncommon in the north, most of the area was uninhabited. Even in the towns the parishes were small, as can be seen in the City of London, and at such places as York and Cambridge to-day. Each parish was a settled community in which ties of blood-relationship played a very important part. It contained representatives of different social classes and different occupations. The ideal that the incumbent of the church should know all his parishioners, at least by sight and name, was not impossible of attainment. To a very large extent all this was swept away in the nineteenth century. Within a radius of (say) five miles from the centre of almost any town the parochial system was overwhelmed as it were by an avalanche. Almost

## THE CHURCH IN THE NINETEENTH CENTURY 101

in a night the old village community became a suburb containing several thousand people.[1] The new settlers had no natural cohesion, and were divorced from all the traditions which had formed the background of their parents' lives. They had no status and no roots, and most of them were desperately poor.

Walter Farquhar Hook (Vicar of the Parish Church of Leeds 1837–59) was the first person who made an effective effort to grapple with the situation. He set a standard which has been maintained by his successors ever since and followed in many other places. Between the years 1840 and 1890 fifty churches were consecrated in Leeds. Five or six of them replaced older ones which had become too small. The rest were new foundations. (I mention Leeds specially because it is the place of which circumstances have enabled me to know most. What went on there illustrates what was happening at the same time in all the principal centres of population.)

It may be doubted whether justice has been done to the overwhelming difficulties which the course of events forced upon the Church during the nineteenth century, or of the magnitude of the effort which was made to overcome them. If it was not fully adequate, it was on the heroic scale. Unfortunately, most of the Victorian church builders did little or nothing to endow their foundations. They did not foresee that without considerable endowments it would be difficult, if not impossible, to provide an adequate staff of clergy for them. Money for the purpose could have been found more easily then than now.

The general outlook of the Church at the beginning of the period was the product of the Evangelical movement of the eighteenth century. That laid hold of England as nothing had done since the coming of the Friars more than five hundred years before. It began with the lower classes, but eventually permeated every stratum of society. There is a good picture of what it meant in the higher ranks in *Vanity Fair*. Sir Pitt Crawley the younger, and his mother-in-law the dowager Countess of Southdown may have been pompous and priggish. Thackeray deliberately makes them rather absurd; especially the countess. But they had real religious and moral principles, which Sir Pitt had certainly not inherited from his father, of which they

[1] This still goes on.

were not ashamed. The value of such people, especially in the demoralized and dissolute society of which George IV was the head, was great. It is to them that we owe, under the leadership of William Wilberforce, the abolition of slavery in the West Indies in 1829, and later, under the leadership of Lord Shaftesbury, the successive Factory Acts, by which the abominable conditions under which people (for the most part women and children) worked in cotton mills and similar places were at least mitigated.

Throughout the eighteenth century there had always been a High Church tradition, represented by such men as Dr. Johnson, which was continued by Dr. Routh (the famous President of Magdalen who died in the year 1854 in the hundredth year of his age and was probably the last man in England to wear a wig) and perhaps Bishop Jebb of Limerick.[1] But it had been a very slender thread.

If the strength of the Evangelical movement lay in its personal appeal, its weakness was its extreme individualism. The Church hardly came within its horizon, except as a convenient arrangement for the promotion of piety of which the Government approved. The Evangelicals seemed to have forgotten that belief in the Holy Catholic Church is part of the Creed. This omission the Oxford Movement set itself to remedy.

The story is so well known that a very brief sketch will be sufficient here. The first stirrings were some private conferences at the rectory of Hadleigh in Suffolk, under the presidency of Hugh James Rose, who happened to be a Cambridge man. But the real beginning is always considered to have been Keble's famous Assize Sermon, *National Apostacy*, which was preached in the University Church at Oxford on 14 July 1833. The immediate occasion was trivial enough.

As the strength of the Reformation had been its appeal to the conscience of the individual, its prospects of success amongst the Celtic population of Ireland had never been bright. The character and conduct of many of the bishops appointed during the seventeenth and eighteenth centuries had done little to improve them. By 1833 the failure was obvious, and a good many of the bishoprics were plainly redundant. Economically they were an intolerable burden on a poor country.

[1] 1823-33.

Accordingly the Government suppressed them. The sees had always been donative; that is to say the bishops had been appointed by royal mandate without any form of capitular election. The Irish Cathedral Churches had no real Chapters which could elect.

It is not clear how much of this was known to Keble. Apparently all he could see was, as the title of his sermon implied, that the Government had repudiated the Christian religion and was dealing with the Church as if it were one of its own departments.

The sermon aroused great excitement, especially in Oxford, and led to the publication of a number of very remarkable pamphlets called *Tracts for the Times*.

The tracts called attention to the fact that the Church of England is not a creation of Henry VIII or Elizabeth, nor a branch of the civil services. It has had a continuous history for more than twelve hundred years, and is a part of something still more ancient, and much larger than itself. It has more in common with the Church of Rome than most Englishmen at that time suspected. All this needed saying, and the tracts enjoyed an immense circulation, which they deserved. The series came to an abrupt end with the publication of the ninetieth. This was by John Henry Newman, who was perhaps the most distinguished of a very distinguished company, which included (amongst others) Edward Bouverie Pusey. In *Tract No. 90* he set himself to show that the Thirty-nine Articles could be interpreted in a sense with which no Roman Catholic need quarrel. The modern reader must judge the reasoning for himself. The storm which this produced showed that this tract had better be the last. In 1845 Newman was received into the Roman Church, and a number of other Tractarians, as the adherents of the new movement were sometimes called, followed his example. Despite this the movement continued to spread. It provoked a good deal of hostility, as its descendant 'Anglo-Catholicism' does to-day. Much of this was ignorant and malicious; some was not entirely undeserved. Foolish aping of Roman Catholic ceremonial and phraseology, and an extremely provocative attitude in the face of any criticism have been, and still are, matters for regret.

On its good side the movement led to a much higher standard of pastoral duty amongst the clergy, and more diligence, care, and reverence in the rendering of Divine Service. It also promoted a higher appreciation of Sacraments, and a better understanding of the position of the Church of England in relation to the rest of Christendom. Great attention was paid to the fabric and fittings of churches, many of which had fallen into a lamentable condition. If some of the 'restorations' of ancient churches which were carried out are more remarkable for the zeal which prompted them than for the knowledge by which they were directed, credit must be given to the authors for their good intentions. There can hardly be a parish in the land to-day which does not owe something to the movement, whether it knows it or not.

In the preface to Dr. Yngve Brilioth's book *The Anglican Revival*, Dr. Headlam,[1] a very distinguished son of Oxford and lately Bishop of Gloucester, has called the movement a failure. This seems to be too sweeping. It is true that it has never taken hold of the nation as its Evangelical forerunner did. It has remained semi-academic, and has affected the clergy much more than the laity. This has tended to promote a cleavage of thought and feeling between them, which the Theological Colleges which have come into being from the year 1840 onwards have done nothing to diminish. This may prove dangerous, as Archbishop Benson foresaw more than fifty years ago. The most dubious legacy of the movement is the particular interpretation which it has put upon the phrase 'Apostolic Succession' in relation to the episcopate. Considerations of space make it impossible to enlarge upon this point here. If the question is asked—'How much of the movement as a whole can be incorporated permanently into the system of the Church of England?' the answer seems to be—'As much as is compatible with the religious freedom and moral responsibility of the individual which the Reformation aimed at securing.'

An important episode was the conflict between religion and science. It began when geologists pointed out that the earth had existed, and men had lived upon it, for a very much longer period than had been imagined. It blazed up when Darwin published his *Origin of Species* in 1859. It was obvious that his theories, or anything like them, could not be reconciled with the early chapters of Genesis, as they were then commonly under-

[1] Died 17 January 1947.

# THE CHURCH IN THE NINETEENTH CENTURY 105

stood, and it seemed to many people that the very foundations of religion were being destroyed.

To us now most of the conflict appears to have been quite unnecessary. The Church has never attempted to define Inspiration, and the protagonists on that side were slow to recognize that what was really being challenged was not inspiration itself, but an arbitrary theory of its nature. This was in fact a comparatively recent growth. The view of the Old Testament which had become general was very different from the one which had been held by the early Alexandrian scholars, especially Origen.

Their opponents did not see that the function of natural science is to describe processes. A description is not an explanation, and as soon as the student of natural science begins to talk of 'Cause and Effect', or to appraise values or point to meanings, he has stepped outside his own province, and is likely to become as sounding brass or a tinkling cymbal.

It seems also to have escaped the notice of both sides that the entire study of any form of natural science starts from the assumption that the visible order is at bottom rational. If it were not it could not be intelligible. If it is not intelligible the study of it is equivalent to trying to extract the square root of a surd. No one need wish to dispute the assumption. But to act upon it is a venture of faith at least as bold as any demanded by religion. It must be admitted that the temper displayed by some of the leaders on both sides, notably by Bishop Samuel Wilberforce and Professor Thomas Huxley, did them little credit.

A more formidable attack came from Germany through the Tübingen school. A group of German divines set themselves to rewrite the early history of the Church on the assumption that St. Peter and St. Paul had been at daggers drawn throughout their lives. The New Testament, they believed, was written about the middle of the second century with a view to concealing this fact, and therefore very little of it (really nothing of Acts) is what it professes to be. These views attracted considerable attention in England. At that time people had not realized that a German can combine wide learning and immense industry with a wrong-headedness which vitiates all his conclusions.

The historical value of the New Testament was at stake; a

very different matter from the historical value of the early chapters of Genesis. It was vindicated principally by three Cambridge scholars, Professors Lightfoot, Westcott, and Hort, the first two of whom were destined to become in succession bishops of Durham. They were all in the first rank, Lightfoot being unquestionably the greatest of the three. Before them English work in this field had been dilettante. They set themselves 'to write something which the Germans would have to read', and they succeeded.

About the year 1865 what were known as liberal opinions began to spread, chiefly in literary circles. Matthew Arnold[1] may be regarded as a representative upholder of them. They owed something to German inspiration, and the gist of them was that the Hero of the Gospel is primarily an ethical teacher. A cloud of legend has gathered round Him, which can no longer be taken seriously. The only religion which educated and intelligent people can be expected to accept is the Christian moral standard, without the supernatural sanctions with which the Church has tried to make it more impressive.

The nineteenth-century liberals did not see that no system of moral teaching will be effective divorced from moral power. We do not need to be told what we ought to do, because we know already. Where we fail is in living up to the best of our knowledge. Our real need is to be given some new power to make new and sustained moral efforts: and to renew them as often as they seem to have come to nothing. Sin and ignorance are not the same thing, and they need different treatment.

These ideas lingered on until after the year 1900, principally in academic circles at Oxford and Cambridge. They were trampled to death by the march of the German armies in the summer of 1914.

Between the years 1840 and 1890 (roughly) Church affairs seem to have attracted much more general attention, especially amongst the educated classes, than they do now. Religious and theological books of a solid character were read and discussed more widely than they are to-day. The best illustration is to be found in a curious episode, the story of which is almost forgotten, so that it will bear repetition here. In the year 1874 a book appeared entitled *Supernatural Religion*. It was published anony-

[1] 1822–88.

# THE CHURCH IN THE NINETEENTH CENTURY 107

mously, but rumour ascribed it to Connop Thirlwall, who had resigned the see of St. David's earlier in the year. The gist of it was that early patristic literature, especially that of the second century, is a collection of forgeries, or at best wholly untrustworthy. Its value for the light which it throws upon the general condition of the Church at that period, and upon the contents of the Canon of Scripture as then recognized, is virtually nil. The author presented himself as a man of wide learning, and the reviewers and the reading public were deeply impressed. Several editions appeared in quick succession. Lightfoot, who was then a canon of St. Paul's, wrote a series of articles which appeared in the *Contemporary Review* at intervals between December 1874 and May 1877. He showed that the author had borrowed freely from the work of others, without acknowledgement, and had sometimes misunderstood what he was reproducing. His knowledge of Greek was scanty. He was, in fact, a pretentious impostor.

The upshot may be told in the words of Dr. Savage, who was a fellow of Corpus Christi College, Cambridge, and subsequently one of Lightfoot's chaplains. Eventually he became Dean of Lichfield.[1]

I remember a conversation in the early 'eighties with a well-known bookseller about Lightfoot's articles, and he told me, in his quiet and judicial way, that they constituted the most remarkable phenomenon in the publishing trade that he had ever known or heard of. 'When the book *Supernatural Religion* appeared', he said, 'it had an extraordinary reception. It was emphatically praised by the reviewers, and its sale was so rapid that the publishers could hardly produce it, in its successive editions, fast enough to meet the demand. But before the series of Dr. Lightfoot's articles was even approaching completion, the book was already a glut in the second-hand market.'

To us to-day it must appear almost equally extraordinary that there should have been so large a public prepared to buy what purported to be a work of real learning (and possessed all the externals of one) and capable of appreciating the cogency of Lightfoot's attack upon it.

During this period churches generally seem to have been well attended, and the standard of preaching to have been high. R. W. Church (Dean of St. Paul's 1871-90) and H. P. Liddon

---

[1] Quoted in *Lightfoot of Durham*, pp. 9-10.

(Canon of St. Paul's 1870-90) are perhaps the two most distinguished members of a goodly company. Liddon's sermons, none of which took less than an hour to deliver, were an event in the life of London. All over the land the pulpit was a real power. There was also a number of exceptionally able bishops. Mention may be made of Tait (London 1856-68, Primate 1868-82), Wilberforce (Oxford 1845-69, Winchester 1869-73), Thomson (Gloucester 1861-2, York 1862-90, Magee (Peterborough 1868-90, York 1890-1), Benson (Truro 1877-82, Primate 1883-96), Temple[1] (Exeter 1869-85, London 1885-96), and Lightfoot (Durham 1879-89). Westcott (Durham 1890-1901), Stubbs (Chester 1884-9, Oxford 1889-1901), and Creighton (Peterborough 1891-97, London 1897-1901) are as it were an afterglow.

After about 1890 the 'climate' began to change. The first and most ominous sign was a decrease in the number of candidates for Holy Orders, which persistent and praiseworthy efforts to extend the field from which they were drawn have done little to remedy.

Another unwelcome change was the decay of the country parsonage. This was due primarily to a combination of economic and social factors. Down to about the year 1900 the country parson was seldom entirely dependent upon his professional earnings. Even when the Tithe Rent Charge fell to not much more than two-thirds of its nominal value he enjoyed a reasonable competence and could give his family as good an education as he had received. A liturgical purist might have found something to criticize in the conduct of his services, and his parochial methods were not in accordance with some modern text-books. But he was respected by his parishioners, and his personal influence for good, supported by that of the well-ordered Christian household of which he was the head, was very great. Not infrequently he was a scholar and kept in touch with his university. Sometimes he produced books of real value. More often than not he was country-bred, and none of the interests of the country-side were beyond his horizon. The quality of the family life of the Victorian parsonage is attested by the number of its sons and daughters who have served their generation well in Church and State; in some instances achiev-

[1] He was translated to Canterbury in 1896, but was really too old for the office.

ing high distinction. A few of them are living still. The almost complete disappearance of clerical homes of this type is a national loss. It is not easy to see how anything else can pretend to fill the gap.

From 1835 onwards the organization of the Church became more elaborate.

The Ecclesiastical Commissioners were created to take over the episcopal estates. The time had gone past when a bishop ought to be personally a considerable landowner. The incomes of some sees were excessive, while those of others were inadequate. Unfortunately, the new figure assigned was regarded as a permanent maximum. The fall in the value of money, due presumably to the discoveries of gold in California, Australia, and South Africa, was not foreseen, and the possibility that an income which was adequate in 1836 might have ceased to be so by 1900 was not taken into account.

In 1856 the Commissioners laid heavy hands upon the revenues of cathedrals. 'Surplus endowments' were removed and used to finance the parochial system, which was being hard pressed by the circumstances referred to in an earlier part of this essay. The immediate relief was great to the parishes, but as a long-term policy the effect upon the religious life of England as a whole may be compared with the effect which might have been produced upon the intellectual life of the nation if universities and colleges had been stripped of much of their revenues in the interest of elementary schools.

In 1836 the see of Ripon was formed: the first new bishopric since the reign of Henry VIII. Other new sees followed—Manchester in 1848, St. Alban's and Truro in 1877, Liverpool in 1880, Newcastle in 1882, Southwell in 1884, Wakefield in 1888, Southwark and Birmingham in 1905, Sheffield in 1909, Chelmsford and St. Edmundsbury and Ipswich in 1914.

Ripon and Manchester were collegiate churches and as such equipped with a dean and canons residentiary already. None of the other new cathedrals, except Liverpool, has been provided with adequate Chapters, and fears are now being expressed that some of the new dioceses, especially those which have come into being since 1914, are too small.

In 1860 the Houses of Convocation were allowed to transact business. In 1717 they had been arbitrarily silenced by George I because they were suspected of being nurseries of Jacobite sentiment. They were not forbidden to meet, but were not suffered to discuss anything; which meant that the formation of any kind of public opinion amongst the clergy was almost impossible. In 1886 a House of Laymen was added to the Convocation of Canterbury, and York followed suit four years later.

In 1861 the first Church Congress was held at Cambridge. This was, as its title implies, a meeting for purposes of discussion only. It had no executive authority and passed no resolutions. Papers on subjects of general interest to the Church were read, often by extremely distinguished authors, and speeches were made. The real value of the institution was that it provided a link between the world of religious scholarship and learning and the rank and file of the Church. Its success was largely due to the fact that it was not tied to London but was held at a different place every year. When the Church Assembly appeared in 1921 the Church Congress ceased to be of sufficient interest to be continued.

About the same time the office of Rural Dean, which had fallen into abeyance, was revived. The periodical meetings of the clergy of a rural deanery, known as Ruri-decanal Chapters, are as a rule of real value and interest. The average extent of a rural deanery is about twelve to twenty parishes.

In 1870 the office of Bishop-Suffragan, which had lapsed in 1607, was revived, and bishops of Dover and Nottingham were appointed to assist the two Primates. Since then these useful functionaries have multiplied to an almost alarming extent. The problem of finding means to support them without appropriating funds intended for other purposes has not yet been solved.

The most remarkable feature of the century taken as a whole is the expansion of English Christianity overseas. While the Church of England cannot claim the whole credit for what was done it made a very honourable contribution. It is impossible to go into details here, but mention may be made of two landmarks.

First the foundation of the Colonial Bishoprics Fund in 1841, and secondly the summoning of the first Lambeth Conference in 1867.

As the former of these was sponsored by the Archbishop of Canterbury (William Howley), and the Bishop of London (Charles James Blomfield), it may fairly be regarded as a corporate act of the Church. Down to that time all our work overseas had been inaugurated by courageous individuals, or by semi-private societies of Church-people. In 1841 the Church as a whole took cognizance of the fact that it had immense responsibilities beyond our own shores.

The fund was inaugurated formally on 27 April by a meeting held at Willis's rooms, King Street, St. James's, over which the Archbishop presided. Before the end of the year six new bishoprics had been established, and the occupants were on their way to them. New Zealand, which has since become Auckland, Valletta (since moved to Gibraltar), New Brunswick, Cape Town, Van Diemen's Land (Tasmania since the name of the island was altered), and Ceylon (now known as Colombo). It is not too much to say that a new chapter in the history of the Church of England was begun.

In 1867 the Archbishop of Canterbury (Charles Thomas Longley) took the bold step of inviting all the bishops in full communion with the Church of England, including those of the United States, to meet at Lambeth for consultation and discussion. One hundred and forty-four invitations were sent and 76 bishops came; 33 from the United Kingdom, 24 from the Colonial Churches, and 19 from the United States. A number of bishops, including the Archbishop of York, refused to come because they thought that the real purpose of the conference was to uphold the action of Bishop Gray of Cape Town, who had excommunicated and deposed Bishop Colenso of Natal for heresy.

The Conference was so successful that it was decided to repeat it at ten-year intervals.

In 1908 242 Bishops were present; 98 from the United Kingdom, 55 from the United States, and 89 from various colonial and missionary dioceses in various parts of the world. Circumstances have prevented the holding of more than two Conferences since that date, but it is proposed that there shall be another in 1948.

The period 1816–1914 was undoubtedly a very great one in the history of the Church and the nation. It has become customary in some circles to belittle the Victorians. The worst that can be said of them is that they cherished a somewhat vague belief in what was termed Progress. No attempt to define Progress was reached, but it was regarded as almost automatic. It seemed self-evident to such a man as Macaulay that if population and wealth were increasing, if travel was easier, and the amenities of life were becoming more abundant, all was well, and getting better every day. He did not seem to see that all these things place an additional tax upon moral character. If character does not develop correspondingly the 'progress' made will be down the slope of Avernus.

It is perhaps true that the Victorians attached too much importance to money, and to the things which money can buy. The modern orator who speaks of 'a higher standard of living' when he means no more than 'a larger amount of material comfort' is helping to perpetuate the worst tradition of a great age, which he probably affects to despise.

The great achievements of the Victorians were made possible largely by the fact that they rated integrity, industry, and thrift very high in the scale of virtues.

The charge of hypocrisy which is sometimes brought against them appears to emanate from people who do not know what moral earnestness is, and therefore cannot recognize it when they see it.

# IX

## A MINIM'S REST

### By R. VAUGHAN WILLIAMS

IN the *Merry Wives*, Act I, Scene iii, occurs the following dialogue:

FALSTAFF: His filching was like an unskilful singer,—he kept not time.
NYM: The good humour is to steal at a minim's rest.

The eighteenth-century wiseacres, knowing nothing of music except as an expensive noise, and never having heard of a 'minim' except as a liquid measure, solemnly altered 'minim' to 'minute' and this reading persisted right into the nineteenth century.

We can learn a great lesson from this apparently unimportant bit of literary editing.

Why could Shakespeare make a joke about a minim's rest and be sure of his laugh, while the eighteenth century did not even know the musical term? Because, under Elizabeth, music was a living thing to old and young, rich and poor. At one end of the scale comes Morley's pupil who was ashamed because he could not take his part in a madrigal after supper, and at the other the 'groundlings' who did not misunderstand when Shakespeare called one of his most beautiful songs silly sooth, old and plain, sung by the spinsters and knitters in the sun. They knew that Shakespeare realized the beauty of their 'old plain' ballads; is he not always quoting them? What would Dr. Johnson have said if he were told that because he had no ear for music he was fit for stratagems and spoils? He refused to smile with the simple and feed with the poor—'Nay, my dear lady, let me smile with the wise, and feed with the rich'.

How came it about that in the eighteenth century music was driven underground except as an exotic luxury for the rich? Well, for one thing we had a German king who brought in his train one of the greatest of German composers, who finally planted his heavy heel on our island music-making. This German king was at the beck and call of a landed oligarchy which grew daily in power and wealth. The sons of these country gentry were sent on the 'grand tour' of Europe whence they returned laden with foreign pictures and sculpture and bringing home with them a voracious horde of French, German and Italian musicians who did not try to understand our art, but planted their own standards in its place. They were at one and the same time worshipped as divine beings and despised as 'damned French fiddlers'—a wholesome state of things in which a national art might flourish!

Music came to be considered a foreign luxury to be enjoyed by the rich, together with their wine and their China tea, but to practise which professionally was entirely unworthy of John Bull. Thus the divergence between art and life grew ever wider. Art became isolated in cathedral closes, parish churches, and Nonconformist chapels. Perhaps this was not altogether a bad thing, for within these narrow confines there grew up the art of the eighteenth-century hymn, psalm, and chant tunes; something entirely *sui generis* and within its limits often very beautiful.

And what about the music of the people which had flourished exceedingly in Tudor times? We know that Squire Western still liked 'Bobbing Joan' while Sophia preferred Mr. Handel. In the end Handel won and the songs of the people were no longer sung in more prosperous circles. The peasantry, owing to the Enclosure Acts followed by the Industrial Revolution, became a depressed class indeed; the iron curtain descended on their activities—but were they dumb? Their music and their poetry were indeed ignored right into the nineteenth century by the manor house and the parsonage. In vain did the squire's daughter and the parson's wife try to interest their tenants and parishioners in the music of Mendelssohn and Spohr—no, they were 'entirely unmusical'. Poor ignorant ladies bountiful! They had only to listen outside the village alehouse or the labourer's cottage of an evening. There, age-old ballads such as Percy would have envied were sung to tunes of a classical distinction and beauty. Woe betide these interlopers if they were seen—the singer would at once shut up like an oyster and become once again 'entirely unmusical'.

George Trevelyan in his *History of England* has a wonderful passage in which he describes the submergence of the Anglo-Saxon tongue unwritten and unspoken except by the villein through three centuries till it emerged in Tudor times as the vehicle of the poetry of Shakespeare and Milton.

## A MINIM'S REST

Is it possible that the same thing is happening with our music? Long it has lain underground. The old psalmody of the parish church was destroyed in the fifties and sixties by the Oxford Movement and *Hymns Ancient and Modern*. The church band was superseded by the wheezy harmonium and later by the American 'organ'. The folk-song ceased to be sung in its true environment after the Education Act, 1870. Why try to make your own music when it can be obtained much cheaper and nastier through the popular press?

But if the light of English music flickered, it never quite went out. Arthur Sullivan had the makings of a unique composer—but circumstances were too much for him. It seems fated that our musicians should be born out of due time. Purcell lived before the great period when his genius could have its full technical equipment. Wesley was tied hand and foot to the organ-stool. Sullivan also was bound by the convention of his time. He could, under happier circumstances, have written another *Figaro*—but 'light' music was obliged to be trivial; 'serious' music had to take on the smug solemnity of the mid-Victorian oratorio. Music which should be at once light and serious was unheard of.

Perhaps the darkest hour was before the dawn. The nineteenth century saw the birth and early development of Parry, Stanford, and Elgar. They were the pioneers who led the way to the great resurgence of music here in England. What was the life-giving power which led these men to hand on the torch of triumph? Time was when music by a British composer meant rows of empty seats. Now all is changed—why? Because all the composers of this renaissance from Parry to Britten, different and often antagonistic as their aims are, have this in common—that they realize that vital art must grow in its own soil and be nurtured by its own rain and sunshine.

But this alone would not be enough. Virginia Woolf writes: 'Masterpieces are not single and solitary births; they are the outcome of many years of thinking in common, thinking by the body of the people, so that the experience of the mass is behind the single voice.'

It takes 1,000 bad composers to make one good one, it takes 1,000 mediocre violinists to make one virtuoso. Some people say that art is for the few—that may be true, but it is only from the many voices that one can pick out the few who know the password.

It was not so long ago that the *Encyclopaedia Britannica* could define Art as an ornament on the fringe of life, a luxury for those who could afford it, and to this day *The Times* classifies a performance of Bach's *Passion* in a church under the heading of 'entertainments'. But the mass of the people have by this time realized that music is not only an 'entertainment', nor a mere luxury, but a necessity of the spiritual if not of the physical life, an opening of those magic casements through which we can catch a glimpse of that country where ultimate reality will be found.

It seems that music, not only in its vague aspects but in its very details was an essential part of the spiritual life of the sixteenth century. It was not for nothing that both Shakespeare and Milton were skilled musicians, or that George Herbert could write:

> Or since all music is but three parts vied
> And multiplied;
> O let thy blessed Spirit bear a part
> And make up our defects with his sweet art.

and make sure that he would be understood. How different from the mere dope of 'Music when soft voices die' in the early nineteenth century.

The Elizabethans experienced a great revival of national consciousness which expressed itself in their poetry and music. Are we experiencing a similar revival? It is not mere accident that during the last war, when our national consciousness became very vivid, when everyone was keyed up to greater and greater effort, the need for music became greater and greater. The time will soon be due for the next supreme composer. He will arise in that community which is best fitted to receive him.

# X
# SPORTING WRITERS OF THE NINETEENTH CENTURY

## *By* BERNARD DARWIN

GOOD writing is good writing whatever the subject and the nineteenth century is rich in good writing on sport, ranging from some of the acknowledged masterpieces of English prose to that which is at least pleasant, racy, and full of vigorous life.

He who tries to treat of sporting writers may be allowed something of a sporting form, and, since none but the hopelessly grown-up can now and then resist the temptation of picking teams, I mean to choose an eleven, or the nucleus of one, to represent the sporting writers of the last century. It is axiomatic that the selector is always wrong and no doubt there will be outrageous gaps. There will, for instance, be no Surtees, for though I believe I can dimly discern why others admire him, I have never got right through one of his books even at the bayonet's point. That is a shameful admission, but after all this is to be my own eleven and I shall stick to it.

The players, to carry on this game of make-believe, will be chosen from a number of different clubs, and though I have my prejudices and my almost complete ignorances, I will try to be fair. To open the innings I shall send in Hazlitt and Borrow, from the Ring, though Hazlitt has another and irresistible claim in Cavanagh, the Fives-player. Each has a glorious prize-fight to his credit, one in the essay called *The Fight* and the other in *Lavengro*, where is also the famous 'turn-up' with the Flaming Tinman. The post of honour at first wicket goes to John Nyren of Hambledon, the General of the side, and in his own field the greatest of all. There will be two other cricketing old gentlemen, the Rev. James Pycroft (of *The Cricket Field*) and the Rev. John Mitford, but their places in the order will be lower, and Henry Hall Dixon, the Druid, shall bat at No. 4. As the least horsy of mortals I cannot be charged with favouritism in his case and nothing shall keep him out, for he is brimming over with the right exciting qualities. Next shall come that great and exasperating man, Thomas Hughes, of *Tom Brown's Schooldays*. He owes his place not merely to the School-house match, though that, as Mr. Boffin would say, is stunning enough. There are further the victory of the old West Country champion at backsword play in the Vale of White Horse, and the account of the Seven-oar at Henley from his *Memoir of a Brother*, both chockfull of go and spirit.

I suppose a third Rugbeian (the Druid was one of Dr. Arnold's boys) must have a place, in Charles James Apperley, who was Nimrod. I grudge it him; he seems to me to owe it to reputation rather than achievement; he could be pompous and solemn and more than a little of a snob, and I sympathize with Surtees who called him Pomponius Ego. Perhaps I am a snob myself and so am a little daunted by his grandeur and his string of hunters paid for by the *Sporting Magazine*. I can salve my conscience by remembering that he wrote the life of Jack Mytton and this gave Virginia Woolf the inspiration for a noble essay. At any rate, in he goes, though in my heart of hearts I would rather have the Squire, George Osbaldeston, on the strength of his autobiography that was only discovered a few years ago. He could tell a plain tale well.

Now comes a difficulty from which selectors are seldom exempt, the question of qualification. What of those who flourished principally in the nineteenth century but survived well into the twentieth? Selectors are not always over-scrupulous and neither shall I be, for there are two that I greatly want on my side. One is Mr. Robert Lyttelton, spirited and vigorous to a degree, if only for his immortal account of Cobden's over in the University Match of 1870. The other is Lord Grey of Fallodon. I am no fisherman, but I cannot leave out one who gives me such a yearning for the naiads of the Test and the Itchen. In particular there is the quite perfect description of a walk across Westminster Bridge in the early morning to catch a train from Waterloo to his Hampshire paradise. Let others praise Andrew Lang and the Tweed, and they certainly deserve consideration, but Lord Grey is going in. So now there are ten chosen, and the eleventh place shall stay open in case of emergencies or afterthoughts.

One obvious criticism of this eleven is that most of them were not sporting writers at all. No more they were, and that is probably why they wrote so well about sport. It was but incidental. They only wrote of it when they had something they very much wanted to say. I do not know whether Hazlitt went to Newbury to see Bill Neate beat the Gaslight Man merely because he wanted for once to see a fight, or whether he had thought of it as a good subject and was already shaping his essay in his head on the coach. At any rate, having achieved it he left well alone ever afterwards. He did himself play at fives and rackets but he touched them only when Cavanagh's death moved him. And so with most of my team; they did not live under the shadow of a daily or even a weekly column. They may be said to have been Gentlemen rather than Players, and, though the professional nearly always wins, yet the amateur has certain advantages. He may sometimes be out of practice but he ought never to be stale.

It was otherwise with Nimrod and the Druid. They wrote regularly on sport for money. The Druid in particular was purely a sporting journalist; he had begun writing for *Bell's Life* when he was still at Rugby, though it may be doubted whether Dr. Arnold knew of it. He well deserves the stately compliment of the *Dictionary of National Biography*; 'all sporting journalists have lit their torches at the Druid's flame'. He was not actually the first of his race, for Pierce Egan had come earlier, and ironically enough enjoyed in his day greater fame. But Egan was but a journeyman and a pot-boiler by comparison, and *Boxiana* has little more than the interest of a curious museum piece. All that now remains to his credit, if it is to his credit, is that with his tappings of claret and the like he invented a language of his own, made up of elaborate synonyms. He was probably the parent or rather the great-grandparent of that strange jargon of 'planting the leather between the uprights' and 'trundling from the gas-works end', now almost vanished, for which we may feel some perverse fondness but which cannot be defended. Now the Druid worked from hand to mouth, for small pay to support a large family; he wrote far too hastily and without revision; yet in his least inspired moments he wrote good and racy English with unflagging spirit, wrote, as Dr. Portman said of Arthur Pendennis, 'if not like a scholar at any rate like a gentleman'. There is to-day a vast amount of writing on sport and games, but among all those who have made it their business in life it is hard to think of more than one who, like the Druid, has produced not merely writing but literature, and has lived regularly up to his own high standard. That one is Mr. Neville Cardus, who would be in a team of all the centuries but comes too late for my period.

It is true that the nineteenth-century writers had one great advantage. They came first, or nearly first. They were not inhibited by the feeling that it had all been said before. When Hughes wrote his account of Rugby football he was describing a game that most of his readers did not know, and so was leading them into a new and exciting world. It was easier for him and his contemporaries to say the simple and eternal things about games, the fire and the dash, the jollity and friendliness of them. Their successors of to-day must needs be more technical, and technicalities do not stir the blood. Even Nyren was comparatively dull in the *Young Cricketer's Tutor*, when he was giving instruction. It was only when he let himself go on the rich personalities of the *Cricketers of My Time* that he showed what could be done and what he could do. A man can write well or ill, no matter what he writes about, but it is scarcely possible to scale the heights about the two-eyed stance or the resisting left hip.

There was something else besides mere priority which made for fine writing. The sporting world was much smaller than that of to-day and was, moreover, split up into a number of tiny, self-contained, almost inaccessible worlds. 'There was no mistaking the Kent boys', said old Beldham to Mr. Pycroft, 'when they came staring into the Green Man.' Kent was to Hampshire a foreign land. Nyren's power of depicting his heroes came from intimate knowledge, from love of his own friends, the companions of his daily life. He gave but a few sentences to their adversaries; all his enthusiasm was spent on his own small circle. It is scarcely possible to write so well, with such a fine frenzy of patriotism, of a wider one. 'Their provinciality in general and personal partialities', said Nyren of the crowd on Windmill Down, 'were naturally interested on behalf of the Hambledon men.' Of course they were, and so were his own, and it is provinciality in this sense that gets the passion into the ink as nothing else can.

We see the same rule still holding good. Mr. Cardus is never so moving as when he writes of his own Lancashire and its Johnny Tyldesley, though he can stretch a point in favour of Yorkshire neighbours. He can picture the elegance of Woolley in skilful phrases, but his Emmott Robinson comes from the heart. I shall never believe that Mr. Lyttelton could have risen so high if it had been Oxford and not Cambridge that did the hat trick and pulled the match out of the fire. He tried bravely over another finish in which Oxford won, but it was not the same thing; something of the divine fire of triumphant hatred was lacking.

E. V. Lucas, Nyren's editor and a true lover of cricket, saw a sign of the times in the fact that such a character as Tom Emmett had been allowed to die without a single tribute to him worthy of the name. The cricketing stage had, he thought, grown too big and too crowded to produce great writing. If this be true, and it is a melancholy thought, it must be true of other games and sports as well, and the nineteenth century is a golden age never to return.

It is worth noting of these old writers that some of the very best of their writing consists in the recording of good talk. Nyren poured out his memories in glowing words and Cowden Clarke, like Dora, held the pens. The exact details of how this partnership functioned may be in question, but there can now be no real doubt as to the respective roles of the two partners. Nyren talked his truly great talk, and Cowden Clarke, allowing himself perhaps a little freedom, wrote it down. If he took any licence he never outstepped its proper bounds, and kept the essential character of talk. 'Upon my life, their speed was as the speed of thought'; we may be sure that those were the old gentleman's very words as he thought in retrospective ecstasy of Beldham cutting.

This was the supremely successful partnership, but it was not the only one. Mr. Pycroft, with Nyren's book in his hand and his 'inkhorn at his button', sought out the survivors of the Hambledon era and set down much that they told him. In Beldham he found a rich mine in which he quarried with devoted skill. The old man's talk was full of notable phrases, picturesque, vigorous, occasionally iconoclastic. They are so vividly impressed with the stamp of truth that we might be sitting with him in his cottage kitchen, as did that other clerical enthusiast, Mr. Mitford, when he put Beldham's bat to his lips for a moment and 'returned it to its sanctuary'.

The Druid provides another distinguished example. To me at least he is never better, never perhaps quite so good, as when setting down the talk of Dick Christian, the famous roughrider of the Quorn country, or of the great huntsmen, Will Goodall and Tom Sebright. He sought them out no doubt as a wise journalist in quest of copy, but he loved them for their own sakes; he gave them their appropriate setting and environment, and made them stand out before the reader, lovable and alive. If he was an interviewer, how truly skilful and sympathetic a one! The journalists of to-day sometimes try to reproduce the words of famous games-players, and the result is sorry stuff. The fault cannot be wholly in the heroes, for character is not dead. This painting of a man through his own words is an art, and the Druid was a genuine artist, 'half sportsman and half poet'. There can be no better illustration of his skill than Dick Christian's account of the fight between Cribb and Molineaux at Thistleton Gap. The old roughrider's ruling passion keeps breaking in; how it was 'stiffish land, a good deal of plough', how he was that day riding a mare of his own for which he had given £80, how the hunt rode over the very spot the day Captain White's Jupiter was killed; 'they all remembered it'. It would have been so fatally easy to hurry the old fellow along, to keep him too closely to the point of the fight, and lose those little touches of nature that make all the difference in the world.

He was equally successful with Will Goodall, who had the gift of phrase and metaphor. 'From Dimbleby they went like pigeons in flight; the horses and even many of our good men, melting away like snow in summer.' Or take this, less picturesque but fully as eloquent: 'We had a regular trimmer! Oh! such a trimmer! which few men live to see.' What immense gusto there is in those few simple words!

Gusto! Oh! such gustos! That is what the reader, and still more he who tries to write himself, must often exclaim in joy and envy and despair. It is the one quality that all these writers have in common, and that in abundant measure. They have it first of all in the sense to be found in the dictionary, in which it is generally used, of zest and enjoyment. They were all, at any rate while they were writing, superlative enjoyers, and had no scruples about saying so. Nyren's lyrical passage in praise of strong ale, 'ale that would flare like turpentine, genuine boniface', comes first, perhaps, to mind; but there are numberless other examples. They relished not merely the game or the sport itself; they were not afraid to embroider, to tell us how they had enjoyed the getting there and the getting back, and all the little incidents that went to swell the feast of happiness. In Hazlitt's matchless fight, the battle itself is but a fraction of the whole. He was at least as happy on the coachtop in a drizzling rain, watching the mile posts go by, or, when he got an inside place, discussing with John Thurtell the mysteries of training; happiest of all sitting by a kitchen fire at Newbury and listening to the yeoman who kept it up all night with endless spirit and talked as well as Cobbett wrote.

There were lesser lights, too, who had this gusto of enjoyment in so high a degree that it made writers of them. There is a hunting description of Bromley-Davenport's, much of which is to me, who have never hunted, quite dull and not always intelligible; but how nobly he breaks out when 'his whole system is steeped in delight, there is not space in it for another emotion'! Such moments bring on a sudden a lovely phrase into his head, as when his horse, approaching a dreaded brook, takes off at exactly the right place and 'describes an entrancing parabola in the air'. He feels that he is flying and his Pegasus, as a rule a comparatively commonplace hack, takes wings with him.

Gusto has another sense in which Hazlitt employs it in one of his essays on painters and painting. 'Gusto in art', he begins, 'is power or passion defining any object'; but it is an impertinence and an impossibility to summarize Hazlitt. All I can do is to give two quotations, both about Titian, which suit my purpose. First he says that 'Not only do his heads seem to think, his bodies seem to feel'. Then, turning to a landscape of Actaeon hunting, 'The winds seemed to sing through the rustling branches of the trees, and already you might hear the twanging of bows resound through the tangled mazes of the wood.'

There, I take it, gusto means briefly the artist's power of bringing a scene to life. It is a power which good descriptive writing must necessarily possess, and the best of sporting writers are very rich in it. How is it achieved? We should all like to know the secret. Largely, no doubt, by the choice of words, so right that they seem the only words possible. Sometimes by a little illuminating detail, as in the account of Cavanagh playing at Copenhagen House, where the wall of the court supported the kitchen chimney; 'when the wall resounded louder than usual, the cooks exclaimed "Those are the Irishman's balls" and the joints trembled on the spit'. In those words he summed up all the joy of hard hitting. But beyond any technical dexterity there is some fervour in the describer's mind which communicates itself to his readers. As a rule it springs from the recalling of something that he has himself seen, but occasionally in his power of imagination, as stimulated by the vision of others. To refer yet again to Cobden's over, the reader would be prepared to swear that the writer saw every ball of it, and heard that satisfying crash of Mr. Marsham's umbrella against the pavilion brickwork as the last Oxford wicket went down. But Mr. Lyttelton was at school at the time; he gleaned his facts from those who had been present and infused his own excitement into them.

If a personal experience may be obtruded, the reporter of golf must range a whole battlefield, on which a number of different fights are taking place simultaneously. He cannot be in two places at once and must rely on others for much that he describes. But if ever he succeeds, to however small an extent, in making his reader feel the agony of a missed putt or the thrill of a great shot, it is long odds that that particular drama has been played before his own eyes. If he has seen no more than 'the 'oofs of the 'orses' through the encircling crowd, he has gained something that the trustiest of scouts can hardly give him. 'It's the hell of a race', exclaimed my old friend, the late Mr. R. C. Lyle, in irrepressible excitement when broadcasting the Derby, and half the old women in England are popularly believed to have written to the B.B.C., protesting against such language. He could not have put half the conviction into his words nor 'got it across' to his listeners as he did, had he not seen that desperate finish himself. There is no adequate substitute for personal vision.

The best writing on games is intensely personal. It is full of the individuality of the writer and of the figure he portrays.

There must be in it at least a measure of hero-worship. This flourishes best in youth, when the worshipped is older than the worshipper, a remote being in a higher sphere. 'Men serve women kneeling. When they get on their feet they go away', and much the same may be said of hero-worshippers. Once our idols are of the same age as ourselves, when we can, with all due respect, address them as man to man, something of the naïve and dog-like quality of our adoration departs. John Nyren was a devout and splendid hero-worshipper, and his religion had come to him early in life, when he would walk to Windmill Down at six o'clock on a summer's morning with David Harris, to see the great bowler choose his wicket. He was an old man when he told Cowden Clarke all about it, but his youthful idolatry came flooding back to him as he talked.

'Fame, after all, is a glorious thing, though it lasts only for a day.' So wrote Borrow, in recalling years afterwards how he had stood on the bowling green and watched the bruisers of England, 'the men of renown amidst hundreds of people with no renown at all, who gaze upon them with timid wonder'. He who writes of sporting heroes must be sure that their fame really is a glorious thing. If he doubts it, if he allows himself to think for an instant that they are beings of very common clay, raised up by senseless idolaters for some trick of skill at a childish game, the magic will go out of his ink. 'Do you see that old man sitting there?' said Mr. Pycroft at Lord's to one of the first amateurs of the time. 'That man is Thomas Beagley.' 'Thomas *who*?' was the reply. That, to Mr. Pycroft, was the profoundest of all tragedies. If it had been anything less, he could not have written half so heart-warming a book.

The writer who feels so intensely the romance of something which to others is perfectly trivial, will now and then go too far. There is perhaps nothing in which the step between the sublime and the ridiculous is so short and so slippery as this kind of writing. Obviously there is a degree of feeling beyond that of which the subject is capable. Perhaps Mr. Mitford went beyond it when he kissed Beldham's bat. I have a horrible fear that he did so when he burst into his valediction to the Hambledon men, 'What would life be, deprived of the recollection of you? Troy has fallen and Thebes is a ruin. The pride of Athens is decayed, and Rome is crumbling to the dust. The philosophy of Bacon is wearing out; and the victories of Marlborough have been overshadowed by fresher laurels. All is vanity but CRICKET; all is sinking in oblivion but you. Greatest of all elevens, fare ye well!' Doubtless a very absurd old gentleman. And yet he was utterly genuine; he lacked neither the brains nor the courage to make a fool of himself, and we may not merely forgive but love him for it.

## XI

## THE CAMEL'S BACK
### or the Last Tribulation of a Victorian Publisher
#### By MICHAEL SADLEIR

GEORGE BENTLEY sat in the first-floor parlour of his lodgings at Tenby, gazing out of the window. It was a french window, opening on to an elegant wrought-iron balcony which overlooked the Marine Parade and, beyond it, the shining sea. As the weather was warm and sunny, Bentley's arm-chair had been set close to the wide-open window, so that he could enjoy the balmy air, watch the modest animation of the Parade, or, if he so wished, doze off to the gentle accompaniment of the wavelets chuckling and creaming over the sands.

He was still in his mid-sixties; but a bowed frame, a bald head and snow-white beard and whiskers, as well as the parchment quality of his skin and his sunken cheeks, gave him the appearance of greater age. Always afflicted with a weak chest, he had also for years suffered increasingly from asthma; and only in Tenby had he found sufficient relief to enable him to face another winter of office work in London. One might therefore almost speak of these comfortable lodgings as his 'Tenby home', seeing that for over twenty years he had paid them an annual summer visit, gathering such strength as he might against the opening of the autumn publishing season and his daily journey from Slough to New Burlington Street and back again.

On this sunny afternoon, although his soft brown eyes were seemingly alert to the holiday traffic on the beach and the sailing-boats scattered here and there about the bay, he saw none of them, being lost in inward reverie. He was a brave man and never prone to self-pity; but his mood at this moment was one of deep melancholy, for he had made up his mind that his career as a book-publisher was over. For the few years left to him (if such there were) he would potter along on the fringe of the business he loved—the business which, in fact, he had largely created. But henceforward Richard, his son, must take command at the office; and he, George Bentley, would remain quietly in the large, comfortable, rather garish house which he had built on the edge of the water-meadows between Slough and Windsor, advising and helping as required, but for the rest re-living the past.

His mind slid back to his youth and young manhood, and especially to his father Richard Bentley the First who had died in 1871 after fifty-three years of publishing, of which the first three were spent in uneasy partnership with that rascal Henry Colburn. George could not help smiling when he thought of Colburn—a regular *petit-maître*, plausible, ingratiating, a rogue to his finger-tips, yet to be admired, however reluctantly, for the irrepressible agility of his intelligence. As a lad in his teens, just started in his father's office in the middle forties, George had seen Colburn more than once; and could see him now, as clearly as though it were yesterday instead of nearly fifty years ago. The shameless little man, despite all that had passed between them, would still call now and again on his former partner, who would receive him with grim reserve, his long thin lips tightly clamped. But nothing could abash Henry Colburn. Dancing on his toes, gesticulating with his hands, fluent in compliment and schemes for mutual advantage, he said his appointed say, while all the time his bright shrewd eyes flickered over desk-top and shelves, on the look-out for any evidence of his rival's plans and progress.

'Poor father!' George thought. 'He was no match for Colburn.' Nor indeed was he. Richard Bentley the First, who in 1819 had gone into business with his brother Samuel as printers on their own account, was a serious, rather unimaginative man, scrupulously upright, and as rigid in his interpretation of other men's duties toward himself as he was of his own obligations toward them. Colburn had been publishing over his own name for more than fifteen years, when the book-trade crash of 1826 swept two-thirds of the publishers of the day into bankruptcy. His account with the Bentley brothers was a heavy one; and they heard with alarm that he contemplated disposing of his business, lock, stock, and barrel and at a knock-out price, to persons for whom the printers had little affection. They took counsel, and in 1829 decided to do precisely what Colburn intended they should do—that is to say, offer to go into partnership with him, and carry the printing account forward to the ledgers of the new firm. Once the Bentley fly was caught in the Colburn web, the spider spun the final strands. Richard, appointed to become Colburn's partner while Samuel continued to manage the printing office, had neither experience of publishing nor detailed knowledge of his new colleague's business. The latter produced a gross over-valuation of his existing copyrights, and on a three-years' agreement secured the profits on the first two years' trading in consideration of his goodwill, estimating this goodwill at a minimum of £5,000 a year. Bentley had to produce working capital in the hope of adequate reward after two years had passed, only to find, needless to say, that most of it went into Colburn's pocket, his famous copyrights proving far less productive than had been stated. In 1832 the partnership came to an end. Richard Bentley appeared as a single imprint and, licking his wounds, prepared doggedly to repair his losses by his own industry and caution.

George thought back to his father's early lists. They were good, conservative lists, and the books were sensibly edited and sensibly produced. The Standard Novels made steady headway, and early in 1837 Richard took a big chance, which might have led to immediate fortune. He founded *Bentley's Miscellany*, with Dickens as editor, *Oliver Twist* with Cruikshank etchings as the inaugural serial, and among other contributions Barham's *Ingoldsby Legends* and work by Maginn, Lover, and a dozen more writers destined to fame.

*Oliver Twist*.... There was a trouble-maker! Was it unfilial in George to feel that, had he been in his father's place, the quarrel might have been avoided? Of course Dickens was impossible—swollen-headed, illogical, totally unable to see reason from any point of view other than his own. And yet the man was a genius, obviously a genius; and to talk to genius in terms of contracts is as futile as to tell a beautiful girl in the excited vanity of a first love affair that she can't go riding with Harry because she has faithfully promised to help Cook bottle the fruit. 'At least,' thought George, 'I could have kept Forster out of it—that arrogant lumbering bully, who fed his own conceit and love of domination on the talent of others! Forster —who began by jilting poor L. E. L. because he heard gossip about her, and ended by marrying Colburn's widow for reasons only too obvious! It may well be I could never have held Dickens; but I do believe I could have parted with him on friendly terms, instead of infecting both him and the firm with a malignant sore which never healed. When at last I was in a position to attempt a reconciliation—and only a posthumous one at that—it was hopeless. It was in 1871, soon after Father died and a little longer after Dickens's death, that Wilkie Collins kindly undertook to approach the Bear with a request for the return of Father's letters. No use. "I enclose copies of the correspondence between Mr. Forster and myself", wrote Collins. "Mr. Forster's answer to my letter makes it, I am sorry to say, impossible for me to represent your views any further. There is some soreness in his mind on this subject, which I do not in the least understand. He has not answered my second letter." That, if you please, to Collins, who had been one of Dickens's most intimate friends.' ('Be honest!' George told himself. 'You know it was precisely this intimacy which soured Forster. I should have known better than to involve poor Collins in so hopeless a quest.')

'Ah well; so it was fated. Thank Heaven "Ingoldsby" kept sweet. The *Legends* were our mainstay during the bad times in the late forties, and have done us wonderfully ever since. Over 400,000 copies in various editions during the last fifty years—there's bread and butter!'

That indeed Barham *had* kept sweet was in itself remarkable. The period of his close association with the firm was in the main before George's time; but the latter had studied the files, and realized how very greatly his father had depended on the genial and diplomatic parson for advice, editorial assistance, and timely intervention when quarrels threatened. The *Miscellany* could hardly have survived without him, apart from his unobtrusive selection and revision of contributions, for Ainsworth, the editor (then in his hey-day), was as touchy as Dickens, and as reliant on Forster for aggressive support against a publisher. Yet Barham handled the vain, capricious Ainsworth with soothing skill, serenely called Forster's imperious bluff, and persuaded Richard Bentley to use soft words, even when hard ones were justified. Barham it was who so rewrote Frances Trollope's *Vicar of Wrexhill* that 'all the revolting expressions were changed or taken out'; who spoke up for Theodore Hook after his death and insisted on a generous and respectful obituary; who, all the time, composed his *Legends* and supplied them for magazine- and book-issue, without ever a sign of vanity or claim to special treatment.

Yet in 1843 Richard Bentley, on the ground of trade depression, brusquely terminated the arrangement by which he paid Barham ten pounds per month for editorial counsel and work, proposing only to continue paying one guinea a page for matter printed in the *Miscellany*. George sighed. Once again, poor Father! He was so often right in the wrong way. Certainly the Bentley finances justified, on strict grounds of prudence, this small economy. But why put it so bleakly? And to Barham of all people, who had given so much of thought and labour to the firm's advantage!

Yet no harm was done. The man was so modest, so truly sweet-natured, that he took no offence, but accepted the cancellation and repeated his undertaking to write for no other publisher. Though two years later he was dead, throughout the forties 'Ingoldsby' was one of the main props of a very insecure business.

The sick man's retrospect moved on. It merely skimmed the remainder of the forties because, during these years of slow recovery from the firm's financial crisis, he had been recurrently laid low by illness after illness. But early in the fifties his health began to improve, and toward the end of 1859 the chest weakness suddenly passed and a second Bentley became a fulltime publisher.

Wilkie Collins—humorous, generous, commonsensical—was the pleasantest memory, alike of those invalid years and of the decades which followed. How well he behaved over the interesting publishing episode of *Poor Miss Finch*! George published this Collins novel in January 1872 in regulation three-decker form. The tale had run—or maybe was still running—serially in *Cassell's Magazine*; and when Bentley's travellers offered the book to Mudie and to Smith, they obtained a negligible response. The Library Despots realized that in two or three months' time a bound volume of *Cassell's Magazine*, containing the whole of *Poor Miss Finch*, would be available at a much smaller price. So their subscribers could wait, the Despots would save money, and Bentley could whistle for his market. Collins immediately offered to return half the money paid by Bentley, and started a roaring campaign against the Despots, which likely enough contributed to the ultimate collapse of the three-decker.

George first came into direct contact with Collins in 1851 (*Antonina*, his first novel, belonged to the young publisher's period of prostration) over the absurd eruption of an unidentifiable bore called Britton. This oddity (Collins called him the 'Venerable Britton') had a book-getting technique of his own.

This is the third occasion [wrote Collins in 1851] on which the Venerable B. has lain in ambush for my books and bounced out upon me with a letter of broad hints. On the first occasion, I gave him a copy of the 'Life of Collins' and received in return a treatise on *Junius*. I couldn't read it, but suppose I ought to consider myself a gainer by my swop. . . . On the second occasion I determined to protect *your* rights of property and evade paying tribute with *Antonina* by writing a polite, grateful and complimentary letter. This answered my purpose for *Antonina* but, as you will see by the enclosed letter, has not protected *Rambles Beyond Railways*. What am I to do? Am I to return a *gift* of illustrations by a *loan* of *Rambles*? Or am I, now and henceforth, to consider the Venerable B. as a sort of second British Museum, regularly entitled to a copy of every book I write? If you decide to send the book, I will toss up with you for the proprietorship of the promised illustrations.

Yes, Collins was a gay, delightful creature and, as such, regarded with suspicion and unease by the conventional relatives and friends of the several authors with whom he was intimate. Forster among them. For there could be little doubt that Forster disliked Collins as a menace to the whitewash he had applied to the Dickens Mausoleum, and for that reason refused (as already recorded) to return Richard Bentley's letters.

George Bentley became co-head of the firm in 1860. His father lived another eleven years and for most of them retained his interest in the progress of the business as he had known it; but dealings with new authors were left in George's hands, and excellent hands they were. George was a true publisher—a man with a genuine feeling for books and their writers, yet with a level—though by no means an asphalted—businesssense. It is only necessary to read the letters addressed to him by author-clients to realize the extent to which he threw himself into their individual preoccupations; and when, as occasionally happens, copies of his replies have been kept in the firm's file, to what infinite pains he went to decide a title or to recommend a textual improvement. Much of the correspondence is naturally concerned with terms of publication; and on this thorny subject one can only admire the mixture of sweet reasonableness and explanatory firmness with which he accepted, postponed, or rejected requests for more favourable treatment.

With the majority of regular Bentley authors relations remained at worst amicable, at best affectionate and intimate. Le Fanu was a good intermediate example. Though a dry unresponsive correspondent, he was essentially a reasonable man. He achieved a startling critical success with *Uncle Silas*, and naturally, viewing prospects from Dublin with only cordial reviews as evidence, concluded that the prices of his future books would show steep appreciation. But good reviews did not necessarily mean large sales, then any more than now. Bentley explained (Feb. 1866) that on *Wylders Hand*, *Uncle Silas*, and *Guy Deverell* Le Fanu had received £750, while the publishers, owing to heavy advertising, had made only £130. The novelist at once retracted his complaint, and they agreed on a further £750 for one two-volume work already serialized in the *Dublin University Magazine* (*All in the Dark*) and one full-length novel to be serialized by Bentley in *Temple Bar* and then published in three volumes (*A Lost Name*). From this time onward Le Fanu, though he had several dealings with Tinsley and Chapman & Hall on account of good serial-payments (which frequently carried book-rights with them), did not cease to be a Bentley author.

Then there was John Leicester Warren, who became Lord de Tabley. He published four anonymous or pseudonymous novels with Bentley in the late sixties and early seventies, and a more modest or considerate man could hardly be imagined. Quite recently a happy chance had brought to New Burlington Street a novelist with whom affectionate intimacy had developed almost overnight—the Dutchman, van der Poorten Schwartz, who wrote as Maarten Maartens. Occasional encounters of this kind made publishing something more than an interesting and varied harassment.

His mind veered to the ladies. He, George Bentley, had had his share of the ladies; and it was to his experience of the last and most overwhelming of them was due his present invalid state. Not that there had not been, among women-writers also, real friends. Dear Annie Edwardes, for example, of whom even her tartest competitors spoke with liking and admiration. And Geraldine Jewsbury. The latter had been another Barham —a devoted editor and reader of manuscripts, though very unpopular with some of her victims. Sometimes the firm's lady-authors exchanged barbed civilities with their fellows via the publisher's post-bag. George well remembered Rhoda Broughton on Miss Jewsbury; and further recalled the same lady's insistence that Clark Russell (who wrote under more than one pseudonym) was a woman—and a disagreeable one into the bargain, that Helen Mathers was a pretentious nitwit, and Hawley Smart a blockhead. Then there was May Laffan who objected to Miss Jewsbury as a reader on grounds of age and prudery; and Miss F. M. Peard who, to the great embarrassment of the publisher, wanted to call a novel *After-Clap*.

Mrs. W. K. Clifford, better than any other, could be malicious and amusing, yet keep her claws sheathed. In March 1888 she had been excellent about Mrs. Humphry Ward:

> I long to read Mrs Humphry Ward's new book *Robert Elsmere*.... The lady is exceedingly clever in many walks of literature but her great ambition is to be a great novelist. She is meanwhile so rough on her sister-scribblers that she is not too popular. Of course it would not matter if she did not review three fourths of the novels for *The Times*, but as she never praises a woman's novel there they cry aloud, all the more as she occasionally slates them also in the Manchester paper—*Examiner* or *Guardian* I forget which. Mrs Hartley (Miss Laffan), who came in for a share of abuse the other day, lifted her voice and declares Mrs W is the Mrs Kemble of literature, which is amusing. *Robert Elsmere* is sure to be brilliant though it may be dull, and it's certain to be praised all round the town.

In February 1892, about her own second novel, *Aunt Anne*, she had written:

> It has no young heroine. It is about an old lady of 68, who falls in love with and marries a young man of seven and twenty. Of

course he breaks her heart and she dies in the end. She is rather a tiresome old thing though she is lovable and pathetic in her way. It would have to be very anonymous indeed for 'Aunt Anne' is alive and her love-making is going apace.

Yes; Mrs. Clifford was good fun, which was more than could be said for several of the others.

On the whole, however, the ladies—entertaining, amiable, or otherwise—were candidly commercial, concerned with terms, re-purchase of copyright, prospects of serial, and so forth. Chief among these was Mrs. Henry Wood, who was never lulled into indifference by her enormous sales. Nearly 450,000 copies of her novels had been sold by 1894, and the demand was increasing. Yet she (or her son) neglected no detail of payment or production nor, during thirty-five years of a Bentley imprint, became more than distantly correct. A strange contrast with poor Mrs. Riddell, who needed money badly but put herself unreservedly in her publisher's hands. The authors of *Misunderstood* (Miss Montgomery), *The First Violin* (Miss Fothergill), and *Diana Tempest* (Miss Cholmondeley) were nearly as fussy as Mrs. Wood, but more confiding and less dictatorial; while Mrs. Hector ('Mrs. Alexander'), like Mrs. Riddell, decided that George was doing his best for her as well as for himself, so stuck to her share of the job and left him alone to get on with his.

It was in July 1885 that a letter reached New Burlington Street from Dr. Charles Mackay, a veteran journalist, poet, and song-writer, which for all its highfalutin seemed innocent enough. Dr. Mackay wrote:

My friend Miss Marie Corelli desires a letter of introduction to you. She is a young lady not only of varied talents but of great genius in the highest interpretation of the word. In an age when there are thousands of women who write verse and think it poetry Marie Corelli towers above them all, writing poetry worthy of the name—poetry such as few women in our day have equalled—I might say none have equalled except Mrs Barrett Browning. Miss Corelli's published poems and prose articles mark her out as inevitably destined, if she lives, to take the highest rank in literature.

Bentley received the young woman, and undertook to consider her first novel, *A Romance of Two Worlds*. The book was accepted and scheduled for publication in February 1886. Then began a flood of letters of which space forbids more than a condensed summary.

First came a brief note about an article for *Temple Bar*. This was followed, on 9 February 1886, by some personal information—romantic though unsolicited:

> I am Venetian and can trace myself back to the famous musician Arcangelo Corelli; and I have a godfather residing in Rome to whom I owe the exceptional severity of the education I have had, first in Italy, next in France, and last and longest in England, which I have learnt to love with a melancholy affection as my mother died here. I am residing now *en famille* with the dearest and best English friends I have.

Marie Corelli was Mackay's only child by the woman who became his second wife; but it seems likely (in view of the letter of 29 January 1890 quoted below) that she was ignorant of the fact, and that her autobiographical pronouncement, over-coloured though it be, was made in good faith.

While *The Romance of Two Worlds* was in course of production, the author is all humility and gratitude; but in April 1886 she makes her first complaint of inadequate publicity, followed in May by criticism of the publisher's advertisement-copy and a touch of the persecution-mania *vis-à-vis* reviewers, which was finally to drive her to withhold review copies of her books altogether. She suggests 'a little thing about the *Romance*', namely, that she thinks the wrong quotes have been chosen for the advertisements. She also explains why the *Morning Post*'s critique was unfavourable. The reviewer came to see her with the notice he had actually written, but declared at the last moment that the wife of Sir William Hardman, the editor, sent in a hostile review which was printed. 'I suppose I shall live down feminine malice some day. It makes me unhappy to incur spite of this kind.'

As the months pass, her letters grow longer. In October she is 'amused to hear that many wise persons such as club-loungers persist in saying I am the daughter of Dr. Mackay. I am quite willing you should say I am his adopted daughter, though no relation.' In November she is the humble little toiler in God's vineyard: 'Don't think I attach any importance to my own work —except that if I *have* done even a small grain of dust of good

I am deeply thankful. The point of the *Romance* was to try to attach scientific possibility to the perfect doctrines of the New Testament.'

Extravagant praise of her half-brother, Eric Mackay, is virtually the only approval of the work of a contemporary. He is a 'wonderful scholar, thinker and poet, and a man of the most manly and modest type. . . . Much more agreeable than Browning whose conceit is simply insufferable.' Among other books of the time, she says of *Diana of the Crossways*: 'Though I like the author *personally* I could never enjoy the book, or master the story which seemed to me very slight.' Rhoda Broughton's *Doctor Cupid* is also 'slight'; William Black's *Green Pastures and Piccadilly* is 'rather weak'; Rider Haggard 'literally wades in blood and savagery' and *King Solomon's Mines* is 'improbable and sickening'; Florence Marryat is 'vulgar and free and easy'; while *Robert Elsmere* 'has absolutely no plot, is calculated to do an immense deal of harm and is a mere echo of a book entitled *Diegesis* by a recreant clergyman, published in 1829. I have the volume. No doubt Mrs. Ward has it also.'[1]

For the time being, apart from dissatisfaction with her share of the firm's advertising space, relations with Bentley are almost fulsome. At an Authors' Society meeting in March 1887 Edmund Gosse attacks publishers, and Corelli thinks 'of my own excellent friend George Bentley, who would have flatly denied any desire to make mincemeat (financially speaking) of me!' She declares her happiness in writing, cannot understand the bitterness of Walter Besant, and dismisses the Society of Authors as 'a mere wasps' nest of grumblers'.

Four days later, on 30 March, comes the first sign of excitement at complimentary remarks from eminent persons. She has been to a fashionable luncheon and met Oscar Wilde, Sir William and Lady Hardman, Mr. Alexander of the Lyceum, and Mr. Forbes Robertson. 'You will perhaps hardly believe that these people had been got together to meet *me*. From one person present who is an *ami intime* of the Prince of Wales it seems that H.R.H. frequently talks about poor me, ardently praising both my books.' This eager response to praise from

[1] This is in April 1888. By February 1892 she has revised her opinion: 'I, personally, think *Robert Elsmere* quite as good as many of George Eliot's. I have read it through four or five times.'

persons of social prominence (as opposed to literary critics) is, in its next manifestation, purely comic. On 14 April she declares that 'two English Earls are carrying on a correspondence with me under assumed names, all about *A Romance of Two Worlds*!' Here, happily exchanging beautiful thoughts with these idiot-noblemen, we will leave Corelli the rising genius. When we catch up with her once more, she will be found sweeping through serious conversations with Mr. Gladstone on her way to dinner with Queen Victoria and the intellectual embraces of the Prince of Wales.

Terms for a new book are the subject of an exchange of letters in March 1887. She asks, for *Thelma*, £150 on publication and £50 after the sale of 700 copies. Bentley replies:

I find that we have made about £30 by *Vendetta*, having expended a very large sum (£200/5/4d) in advertisements. This was owing to my directions to make the book *coûte que coûte*, so that except Miss Broughton's novel, on which the expenditure was still larger, no novel for the last two or three years has cost us so much.

Moreover we had twice to print, the first time 500, the second time 250. Of this reprint we have copies on hand. So that the book was more costly to us than is ordinarily the case, with the result that 656 copies, sold on an average at 15/9d per copy, leave us, as I say, about £30 profit. I do not think you will therefore ask me to depart from the offer I had the pleasure of making you.

She accepts the original offer (see below) by return, but reports approaches, of the vaguest kind, from Ward & Downey and Routledge. In May 1888 she is beginning to be dissatisfied that the sales of her books do not correspond to the compliments paid her about them, and quotes the usual friend who has to wait for days at Mudie's to get a copy to read.

March 1889 sees trouble over the terms for *Ardath*, for which Bentley wants to pay the same as for *Thelma*, viz. £100 plus £50 after the sale of 700 copies plus £50 on the cheap edition. She would like £300 and after the sale of 1,200 copies a royalty of 5*s*. a copy. He resists and they compromise on £100 on signature of agreement plus £100 on publication plus, after a sale of 900 copies, a royalty of 6*s*. a copy. Returning the agreement she reveals that 'in *Ardath* I translated Algazzali's remarks from the Arabic with much earnest pains, even as I did with certain old manuscripts, which through the courtesy of one of the Armenian fraternity at Venice, I was able to consult, and which proved to me that electric light was known and used a thousand years at least before Christ'.

In May there is a slight pother over Hall Caine, who told her at a party that *he* had recommended *A Romance of Two Worlds* to Bentley and graciously accepted her thanks for the service. It was foolish of him not to realize that she would instantly repeat the incident to Bentley, who forthwith rapped Caine over the knuckles and told the Corelli he had done so. He wrote to Caine that on *his* report the manuscript would have been rejected, but that another reader—a woman—thought it had possibilities and suggested the publisher read it himself. Which he did. This incident was, in all likelihood, the starting-point of the bitter rivalry between Corelli and Caine which inflamed the years of their respective best-sellerdom.

The cheering news that 'my brain is very rich in creative fancy (thanks to the Supreme Giver of all these exquisite intellectual emotions) and *Ardath* has not exhausted me' is followed, early June 1889, by a cry of ecstasy: 'Amazement sits upon my brow, my dear Mr. Bentley! Gladstone—the celebrated G.O.M. called upon me *in person* this afternoon!! I was out—so he left his card with his regrets at not seeing me written upon it', and signs herself: 'Yours, still in a state of amused wonder.'

Two days later (5 June 1889) a very long letter describes a second, and better-timed, visit from the G.O.M. Her heart beat; she was even more nervous than when she first saw her publisher. But the gentleness and outspoken admiration of Mr. Gladstone stilled her qualms; and when, after a visit of two hours, he left her, she quickly noted down for verbal transmission to Bentley those of his remarks which pleased her most. She was 'a thinker of no ordinary calibre as well as a perfect mistress of the pen'; she had before her 'a great career'; while 'an earnest woman thinker is more likely to gain a quick insight into the problems of her time than a man, because first, she is by nature sympathetic, secondly because she has such amazing instinct, thirdly because, if virtuous at all, she is certain to be sublimely unselfish'. All this, and a good deal more.

Pleas for more advertising, reports of offers from America and Europe, indignation that Marion Crawford should have had £1,000 for *Marzio's Crucifix* ('Oh, *what* a feeble story!') occupy the weeks until her departure for Switzerland late in August. Then, to the publisher's relief, comes a lull in the correspondence, nothing occurring until October, when she writes from Holland giving the first news of *Wormwood*: 'a strange and terrible phase of the present life of the Paris people ... much more powerful than *Vendetta*'.

Late in 1889 Dr. Mackay died; and she dramatizes to the utmost the last hours, and her own share in them. There is, however, a note of genuine feeling in a letter from Eastbourne written on 29 January 1890:

I may truly say I have been in ignorance of my own history up to lately. Anyway I think it is but fair to tell you that, if you ever wish to know the history of my relationship to the dear old man who has gone, I will sincerely tell it to you, *though to do so*, will possibly seem to cast a slight aspersion on the memory of him and of my dear, sweet beautiful Venetian mother. ... Any question *you* choose to ask shall be frankly answered—there are 'romances' in every life, though not till ten days or more ago, did I know there was *such* a romance in mine.

The early months of 1890 bring comments on various writers. Of Ouida she speaks with perceptive admiration. 'Poor old lady! She has lost all her good fortune. I do not say it is not her own fault, but with all her mistakes she is a brilliantly gifted woman. ... I am sending you *Bimbi* and think you will acknowledge the delicate genius that could imagine these child-stories. She has been deeply wronged by the critics generally.' But Kipling comes off badly: 'Who in the world is Mr. Kipling? I am in the dark as to the Kipling "genius", but I can believe anything of English critics, especially after they undertake to elect that terrible old Ibsen into a sort of fictitious Shakespeare!' This is on 16 April. On 30 April (having 'read his productions with surprise and disappointment') she declares: 'Rudyard Kipling is a young mushroom growing on the roots of the Savile Club'; and on 23 May she has heard from Ouida who 'also wants to know who "Rudyard Kipling" is (with much satire in her way of putting the question)'.

But in early August the shortcomings of Kipling are forgotten in the outbreak of frenzied negotiation and self-justification over *Wormwood*, whose original title was *Gall*. As regards terms she has been offered £500 'by an excellent firm', the copyright to remain hers. Her minimum from Bentley is £400. He, it appears, wishes to repeat the terms on the last book; and a contract on these lines provokes an indignant letter from Interlaken, formally addressed to the firm and not to George Bentley himself: 'Herewith I beg to return the two copies of the proposed agreement, as the terms therein stated are *entirely inadequate*, and are very considerably less than the offers made for the new work by several other publishing firms.'

The letter goes on to reiterate a favourite grievance—that John Strange Winter gets more for a shilling railway novel than Corelli for three volumes of serious well-doing.

On this occasion she wins the day and secures £100 on signature and £300 on publication for 1,500 copies in firstedition form during a period of one year. Thereafter 6s. per copy. For the tenth time she demands why Rhoda Broughton should be better paid; and Bentley patiently explains that his firm buy the Broughton copyrights and, in consequence, naturally pay a larger initial sum. She admits she had not realized this, and slides off into Marion Crawford who 'by some occult means or other gets £1,000 for every book *between* England and America'. May she try her hand at placing *Wormwood* in America? But Bentley must await a Harper option.

He, meantime, is alarmed at the reception *Wormwood* is likely to have from the reviewers and, unwisely admitting this, receives a ferocious counterblast. When has the Press lost an opportunity of insulting her and denigrating her work—the same Press which 'deifies a Rudyard Kipling and hovers between fits of ecstasy and approbation over Zola and Tolstoi and Ibsen'? She puts her reputation (and presumably also her sales) in the hands of the public 'who has always forgiven my sins', and asserts that her exposure of French national decay, 'of the absinthe trail which lies all over France and makes French literature obscene and French art repulsive' is powerful for the same reason that *Père Goriot* is powerful—because, had 'a lurid picture been painted in soft colours', it would have failed of its purpose.

Harpers do not take up their option, and Corelli, who had declared herself possessed of a firm offer of £60, finds, now she can accept it, that it is after all only £25. The disappointment is blamed, with peevish resignation, on the delay caused by waiting for Harpers' decision. For the first time one is conscious of grit in the wheels of her business relationship with her publisher, and the consciousness grows. She is angry over the production, without request for revision, of a one-volume *Wormwood* and over the absence of a special agreement. There can be little doubt that the firm of Bentley slipped up on these points and that her irritation is justified; but the clash leads her directly to threaten to go elsewhere and, unmistakably, to mean it.

The hint of friction (it is little more), though soon lost in a renewal of amiability, was none the less a portent. From now on, the level of friendliness dips more frequently to dissatisfaction and, each time, a shade more deeply than before. But for a while the sun shines. George Bentley, rather foolishly, starts a letter 'Dear Thelma'. She is enchanted, but says with coy significance: 'I am, alas, a long way behind the perfections of my *submissive* ideal Norse heroine.'

Then occurs the bizarre incident of the special binding for the Queen. The Duchess of Roxburghe writes an admiring letter and indicates that a copy of *A Romance of Two Worlds* might be accepted by Her Majesty. 'Thelma' loses no time. On 14 August 1891 she writes to ask 'how soon it would be possible to get a "special" copy for Her Majesty ready, bound in royal red morocco, with the English coat of arms and V.R. underneath? I know you will be as pleased as myself that the book should be in the sovereign's hands'. Excitement grows and her affection for Bentley with it. 'My dear friend (for I know I may call you so)', she begins on 29 August, 'You will see by the enclosed that the Queen actually seems to be *impatient* about my book!'

The enclosure is a letter to the Duchess of Roxburghe from a lady-in-waiting, with a message added by the latter that H.M. may accept copies of other novels also. This, Corelli thinks, should appeal to 'a *loyal publisher*! especially under the rather especial circumstances, and your firm being "Publishers to the Queen" too'.

But, within a week, catastrophe. Telegram:

                                                           Sept. 4, 1891

HORRIBLE BLUNDER BAIN HAS SENT THE BOOK FROM HIMSELF DIRECT TO BALMORAL BY PARCEL POST    NOTHING COULD BE WORSE ETIQUETTE I AM MOST DISTRESSED                                        CORELLI

The affair drops out of sight until January 1892 when, to Bentley's astonishment, the account for the special binding is returned to him with a protest, half-shocked, half-contemptuous. 'Of course I have no objection to pay for the binding of Her Majesty's book, but the honour of the Queen's acceptance is as much yours as mine.... You are Her Majesty's publishers too—altogether it is almost comic!'

To which George Bentley replies:—

You ask me about a charge which appears in your account for binding a copy of one of your books for the Queen. I do not blame them in Burlington Street for making this charge as some authors are very punctilious on these points. They might naturally think you would wish to pay, as the present was your own to Her Majesty.

If you do not share my feeling in this matter, let me know the amount and I will send you my personal cheque, as I can hardly ask the firm to make any alteration in their books.

Who finally paid does not transpire; but Corelli was right in thinking that, with the Duchess of Roxburghe's help, she might attract the attention of the Queen. An invitation to spend a night at Windsor and dine with H.M. is reported in March[1]; but her jubilation is deflated by Bentley's blunt refusal to splash the Royal acceptance of a special copy of a Corelli novel in press advertisements. The lady is bitterly disappointed. 'I feel this lack of sympathetic interest keenly,' she writes on 15 March 1892, 'as I know, and everybody knows, that if the Queen had sent for the first issued copy of Mrs. Ward's book, the fact would have been taken up by her publishers and chronicled in every paper in England.' Bentley patiently explains that H.M. had not 'sent for' *A Romance of Two Worlds* and, further, that he had consulted Sir Henry Ponsonby, who (not surprisingly) declared it out of the question that the Queen's private interests should be used for publicity purposes.

'Thelma' is totally unable to appreciate this obvious piece of good manners. By return of post she promises to 'let H.M. know what unnecessary obstacles are flung in a poor author's career, even when she *has* won the royal favour'; and after repeating some of the Queen's remarks at third hand—via the lady-in-waiting and the Duchess of Roxburghe—ends by

[1] Did the visit ever come off? It is not mentioned again, and one would not expect Corelli to pass it over in silence had it taken place.

disposing finally of 'Sir H—— P——, who is not "in" the matter at all, which perhaps he does not like'.

The correspondence now becomes fractious. Terms for *The Soul of Lilith*; the stupendous earnings of Mrs. Humphry Ward in comparison with her own;[1] accusations that the firm contradict their own reports of sales ('I will send you your own letter if you like'), which accusations are withdrawn when she rereads the letter and finds Bentley said something entirely different; fury at a review in the *Pall Mall*, which tears *Lilith* to pieces and ends: 'The one really remarkable feature of Miss Corelli's achievement is that amid all her absurdity she should contrive to be so dull.' Finally, in sorrow not in anger, she determines to write no more ('I have no heart for the business; *it is not worth it*. To judge by the way some critics write of me I might be the "vulgarest" minded old woman that ever wrote "trash" for her daily bread'), and winds up with a plaintive—maybe an uneasy—reference to a possible suspicion in the minds of jealous critics that she 'had voluntarily toadied to H.M. to get her notice'.

On 20 June 1892 'a well known firm of publishers' offers her £500 for a two years' run of *Lilith* in a cheap edition. She had written to Bentley on 5 May that she wished nothing done about a cheap *Lilith* at present ('it will rest with the result of certain operations now in hand'); but she now sends a copy of the other firm's letter, and accuses poor George of 'indifference' to the book's interests. He replies:

June 24, 1892

You gave me to understand that you did not wish anything done with *Lilith* until you had made up your mind about it. As a consequence I have never troubled you on the subject, which you now construe as indifference.

I cannot be indifferent as you should well know, but I am naturally unwilling to incur a *certain* loss, which would arise were I to give you £500 for a two years' lease of a 6/- edition of *Lilith*. £500 represents the royalty on 10,000 copies. *Wormwood* has sold a little over 4,000 copies, *Ardath* between 5 and 6,000. If *Ardath* has not reached 10,000 copies in 2 years *Lilith* will not, though it is a work of great originality. I think, considering how *Lilith* was launched (you once wrote 'nobly') I ought not to be called 'quite

[1] 'Someone' has told her Mrs. Ward received £16,000 for *David Grieve*!

indifferent' to *Lilith*'s fate. If I advise you to take the £500, it is right that I should do so. I have no wish that you should sacrifice your interests to mine.

The cloud on the horizon is growing.

In August she goes to Homburg, and we read, with fascinated horror, an account of her contacts with the Prince of Wales, who is charmingly informed, talks admirably, walks with her in the garden listening to the music, and declares: 'You are the only woman writer of *genius* we have.' The rest of the letter records an intended drive to Frankfort which was spoilt by rain; the tolerant civility shown by H.R.H. to 'Labby'; and the capture of royal favour by Eric Mackay (thanks to Thelma) which takes the form of a request for a free copy of a book of poems.

Fresh and serious trouble is soon brewing. Late in 1892 appeared an anonymous work called *The Silver Domino*, with which, after a few months, Corelli's name became connected. In the course of the collection of satirical papers ill-natured reference is made to the firm of Bentley. George is much pained, and in the early summer of 1893 writes to say so. She replies at great length and, at first, in a mood of injured dignity. Only 150 pages of the book are by her and the offending ones are not among them. Her explanation of the book's origin is confused and evasive. (Someone unnamed, to whom unsolicited she had shown some satires written and put aside, offered to buy them outright, intending to use them, without mention of her, in conjunction with work of his own.) And as the interminable letter proceeds, she works herself into a state of pained resentment against Bentley, which is so unreasonable as to be suspicious:

None of my *friends* supposed me to be the sole author of the book—only my enemies and—I regret to say—my publisher, who should have known better. . . . I have 'taken no steps to dissociate myself' from the affair, as my doing so would only make matters worse, increase the sale of the book which has already run through eight editions, and attract more attention. . . . Of course I shall not trouble you with my new work, as you have chosen to misjudge me *without even asking for an explanation*, but at once taking *rumour* for *complete fact*. . . . I can but imitate the example of the Queen, who when she is vilely attacked and misjudged by spiteful journalists, is compelled, by the dignity of her position, to keep silence.

L

To which the publisher replies:

Dear Miss Corelli,                                               July 10, 1893

In reply to your letter I should do scant justice to your abilities, if I thought that your account of the reasons which kept us asunder 'satisfied' your conscience. As you are not prepared to take the only course which can set matters straight, I trust that you will not prolong a correspondence which is, I should imagine, as painful to you as it is to me.

Four months later Methuen publish *Barabbas*. The Corelli-Bentley alliance is at an end, but not yet the bitterness which the parting is to engender. For a while she, at least, is happy. She sends George a copy of *Barabbas* with a flowery inscription; she reports the excitement in clerical circles and the sale of 1,000 copies in three volumes and, later, of 10,000 in one volume; she defends herself against his charge of vulgarizing the sufferings of Christ on earth, comparing her book to pictures of the Crucifixion 'worked out by all the old painters in an exalted spirit of love and devotion'; she goes to Florence and is printed next to the Queen in the column of 'arrivals'. Then, in May 1894, she complains angrily that a letter from Lord Dufferin, addressed to her at New Burlington Street, has not been forwarded as promptly as it should have been. George Bentley sees his chance and writes with gentle irony:

Dear Thelma,                                                 May 5, 1894

I am sorry for the delay in the delivery of Lord Dufferin's letter.

But, little lady, you must not be offended if I tell you that whenever any author avails himself of the privilege of using his publisher's office as a post office, it is generally for a brief period, and not over many years, and he generally sends for his letters.

You have over many years had your letters reposted to you, and so many that my clerks have frequently called my attention to it, but as you know I have never asked you to have them sent direct to your own house.

I think that it will be better now that this should be done, the more so as you are once more at home.

This finds its mark, and she protests indignantly that all letters addressed to her at Bentley's office, with the one exception of Lord Dufferin's, have been from total strangers—fan-mail, in short.

And now the final storm is about to break. On 8 June 1894,

having requested the average annual sale of all her books lumped together and an idea of the proportion of the total sold to the Colonies, she designates the figure of 16,000 copies per annum as 'very little, seeing that Methuen have sold nearly that number of *Barabbas* in eight months'. Bentley estimates that a quarter of the total may have gone to the Colonies and she exclaims: 'One quarter would be 4,000 copies of *all* my books—less than 700 copies of each separate novel—for all Australia, New Zealand, Africa, etc.!' She then produces a prize specimen of the 'reliable authority' or 'well-informed friend' on whom credulous and swollen-headed authors traditionally fall back when in conflict with their publishers, and whose evidence, if it be accepted, implies that the publishers' statements are falsifications.

This knowledgeable acquaintance is 'a gentleman connected with a large publishing and bookselling firm in Melbourne', who is in a position to state categorically that her sales in Australia alone are 'larger than those of *any* living English writer of fiction'. He has promised to support his statement by actual figures—'this, because he has taken a great personal liking to me'. She considers that Bentley should be selling her works at the rate of about 100,000 per annum and asks George, as head of the firm, personally to investigate the accounts as rendered.

He restrains himself, and merely expresses regret that her letter was not a 'pretty one'; receiving, almost by return, the following: 'I'm afraid I did not think when I wrote to you whether my letter was "pretty" or not: I was only conscious of an immense surprise that my one book *Barabbas* should sell more in eight months with Methuen, than all my *six* books together with you in a whole year! And the surprise still remains. . . .'

Then, probably not realizing the enormity and absurdity of her words, she accuses the firm's accounts of obscurity, inexactitude, and self-concealment behind a fog of technical detail. 'I must evidently wait till I get the yearly estimate known to my Australian friend who, having invested a large amount of capital in the Colonial publishing firms, is able, he says, to give me the average sum total of the number of my books sold in Australia per annum.'

Bentley no longer conceals his anger, but makes one more attempt to explain the complex mechanics of export sales.

June 16, 1894

Dear Mlle Corelli,

It is natural that the new book should, for the moment, eclipse the permanent sales of all your former books, for we always sell a large number of a *new* book of yours to start with. If you will refer to the accounts you will find that all of your works which go direct from us to the Colonies are there stated. Over and above these copies, other copies go from the large Town houses who buy for all the world. The particulars of such sales, whether to Paris, Melbourne or Calcutta, we know nothing about, but you get paid for them as they are embraced in Town sales.

Your Australian friend's impressions can at least only be guesses, nor do I see what value they have for you, when you have the accounts themselves.

Yours very truly,
George Bentley.

Her reply, and the response which it immediately elicited, are the last letters exchanged between the parties. Corelli's letter is dated 8 July 1894 and begins by reiterating that her six Bentley titles 'make a miserably small appearance' in comparison with Methuen's solitary *Barabbas*, already in its ninth edition and racing toward its tenth. She cannot accept Bentley's statement that his firm does not know how many copies of a book sold to general wholesalers actually go to Australia. 'It will be interesting and useful to me to find this out. . . . I cabled to Melbourne last week and the letter is on its way. Whatever the statements are, they will be *as exact as possible*.'

To the implication of these (and many other) observations only one answer was possible. Here it is.

July 9, 1894

Dear Miss Corelli,

Will you kindly address your purely business letters, such as the one which is now before me dated Sunday July 8, to New Burlington Street. I have carefully read your letter and can come to no other conclusion, in spite of your recent letters, than that you doubt our accounts.

If therefore you will authorize the expenditure, we will call in a chartered accountant, who shall render you a certificated account.

I beg to remain,
Yours truly,
George Bentley.

Thus terminated the eight-year relationship between an author destined to enjoy an immense (if transient) popularity, and the ageing publisher who had financed and guided the first phase of her literary life.

On him the effect of her final insult was crushing; but she, in the heady excitement of her mounting success, had within a week forgotten the whole episode. She bore no grudge nor felt any shame, being unable to understand how deeply she had wounded him. She did not mean to wound; there was no malice whatsoever in her colossal vanity; an impulsive, good-hearted but fundamentally stupid woman, she failed all her life to realize that to be convinced of one's own genius is not enough. Years later, when she herself was on the downward slope, she paid bitterly for her innate and well-meant, but insensitive, absurdity. In 1894 the bill had to be met by George Bentley. And it helped to finish him.

Racked with asthma, he left London immediately for Tenby, where we first encountered him sitting wearily at his window, with phrases from the intolerable outpourings of this intolerable egotist flickering across his mind.

Not the least bitter element in the whole affair was that *on results* the firm of Bentley had been outdone by Methuen. That was sheer bad luck. *Barabbas* was the first Corelli novel to have anything like a sensational sale. Nothing Bentley could have done would have pushed the earlier books into half its circulation. But this no publisher could explain to such an author as Corelli. She set the figures side by side and, regarding all her works as of equal irresistible appeal, concluded that her old publishers were negligent or worse and her new ones brilliantly endowed.

George Bentley was a sick man, already bowed beneath a load of worry and physical frailty. The dispute with Marie Corelli, though it did not, independently of other misfortunes, break the camel's back, did its share. A year later he was dead.

Thanks are due to Mr. Medley of Messrs. Field Roscoe and to Mr. A. S. Watt of Messrs. A. P. Watt & Son, for permission to quote from hitherto unpublished letters from Miss Marie Corelli.—M.S.

## XII
## THE PERFECT AUTHOR

*By* S. C. ROBERTS

IT was one of those rare afternoons when I felt that I could justifiably spend half an hour in doing what the young aspirant conceives to be the regular occupation of the publisher. A manuscript that promised to be of some interest had reached me that morning, so I turned my chair to the fire and sat back with my feet on the fender. The manuscript seemed likely to fulfil its promise and, the office being unusually quiet, I became absorbed in my reading. But the peace was too good to last. The telephone tinkled—gently, it is true, but the spell was broken. The voice of the girl at the switchboard was tiresomely indistinct. Someone wished to make an appointment.

'What's the man's name?' I asked irritably.

'Mr. Cooper, sir.'

'Hooper? Never heard of him.'

'No, sir, Cooper—Mr. Marmaduke Cooper.'

'Heavens!' I ejaculated. 'What's he want?'

'He wants an appointment, sir.'

'Well, put me through to him at once.'

'But he's here, sir.'

'Where?'

'In the waiting-room, sir.'

This was tremendous. For Marmaduke Cooper was, in my view and in that of many others, the most distinguished and the most elusive prose-writer of the time. Articles of his had appeared, at irregular intervals, in monthly and quarterly reviews, and one or two publishers, of the more discerning sort, had approached him with suggestions for a book. But they had failed. Marmaduke Cooper lived in an obscure village in Huntingdonshire, seldom went to London, and protested that he would never write anything suitable for publication in book form. But we knew better. Cooper's prose had a fine, astringent quality that differentiated his work from the journalist's accumulation; there was substance, too, in his essays, and if, occasionally, they showed signs of becoming unduly solemn, a touch of quiet, ironical humour quickly restored the balance. In imagination I had often designed a title-page for a work by Marmaduke Cooper. And now, here he was in my waiting-room.

'Send him up at once,' I said; 'no—wait a minute. I'll come down.'

In the waiting-room I found a quiet little man, poring over some of the new books.

'Mr. Cooper?' I began.

'Yes, yes,' he replied, 'but this is too kind of you. You see, I happened to be in Cambridge to-day—in fact, I expect to be here more than once in the course of the next few weeks. I am anxious to verify some rather obscure references in the University Library and it occurred to me that I might arrange to see you at some later date—just for a few minutes, because I know how valuable your time is.'

'But why not come up to my room now? I am entirely at your service.'

'Really? But are you sure? I really have no right—and, believe me, I had no intention—to interrupt you in this way.'

'Not at all, not at all,' I murmured lamely as I led the way upstairs.

'What a delightful room,' Mr. Cooper exclaimed, 'and what a number of interesting books you have published lately—and at such reasonable prices.'

This was very soothing, but I didn't want to talk about other people's books. I decided to plunge.

'And have you brought me a book of your own to be added to them?' I asked.

'Hardly that. But I will confess that it was about the possibility of publication that I wished to consult you. You see, I have never written a book and I daresay I am too old to begin. But one or two friends have said kind things about some of my occasional essays and so I have felt encouraged to write some more; and, when I had completed them, it seemed to me that, having in fact a continuous theme, they might be more suitable for publication as a book than as separate essays.'

This was unbelievably promising. The most I had hoped as I led Mr. Cooper to my room was that he had changed his mind and decided to collect his essays into a volume. But now he was talking about a new series, all unpublished.

'This interests me very much, Mr. Cooper,' I said; 'I suppose you haven't got the manuscript with you?'

'Well, not exactly. I have a typescript in my little bag, but it is very untidy, I fear. Not what you would call "clean copy". I have found it necessary to make some extensive corrections by hand, but when I have verified certain references, I shall of course have a fair copy made. You see, although I do not for a moment pretend that this is a serious piece of historical work in the academic sense, it does contain a number of quotations from various authorities, ancient and modern, and I am anxious that they should be textually accurate.'

'Of course, I quite understand that,' I said. I was itching to get hold of the typescript, but Mr. Cooper sat placidly with his little attaché-case on his lap.

'And have you given your book a title?' I asked.

'Ah, there you touch upon one of my many problems. I have had great difficulty in finding something suitable. I had thought of "Essays in Rural Philosophy" or something of the kind, unless perhaps it is a little pretentious to introduce the word "philosophy". I am no metaphysician, I fear.'

'You needn't worry about that in Cambridge.'

'You think not? You see, although I have lived, very quietly, in the country for a number of years, I am not in truth a countryman. I am really quite ignorant of farming and harvest-customs and cottage-craftsmanship and what is generally called country lore. To me the value of living in the country lies largely in its detachment. The problems of our civilization are in the cities and I find that it is only from a distance that I can clearly contemplate them.'

'I see. But may I not look at the work itself?'

'Oh, certainly. But I really feel ashamed to show it to you in its present condition.'

'I expect I have seen many worse,' I said. And indeed I had. The typescript contained a good many additions and corrections, but they were all perfectly legible. It was good 'copy' for any decent compositor. I turned over the pages. Even as I did so, my eye caught one or two phrases in the authentic manner of Marmaduke Cooper—firm, clean sentences with just the faintest touch of irony, a manner, as frequently happens, entirely different from the writer's conversational style. I felt that it was time to come to the point.

'And are you thinking of offering it to me for publication?'

'Oh, no.'

My face fell, no doubt. But Mr. Cooper was quick to explain.

'I mean, not at this point. You see, I had no intention of doing more to-day than make an appointment. Then, I thought that, if you could spare the time, I might, on my next visit, ask your advice about the whole question.'

'But why not ask me now? Have you a particular publisher in mind?'

'Hardly that, my dear sir. But a friend of mine, who has much experience in these matters and is, I believe, a prominent member of a body called the Society of Authors, strongly recommended that I should put myself into the hands of a literary agent.'

'But you came to me instead?'

'Well, frankly, I didn't properly understand all that my friend tried to tell me about contracts and advances and options and subsidiary rights and so on. And as I wished, in any event, to spend some time at the University Library, I thought that, while I was here, I might venture to ask you to enlighten me.'

'With pleasure, Mr. Cooper. And as you have done me the honour of asking for my advice, I will give it without delay: Forget the agents. Let us publish your book for you here.'

'But, my dear sir, you haven't read it.'

'That is true, Mr. Cooper. But I have read and re-read your published articles with continuous pleasure and, while we have been talking, I have read the preface, the list of contents, and several paragraphs of your new book. My advice is that we settle the terms of publication here and now.'

'Really?' said Mr. Cooper incredulously. 'You astonish me. But I'm afraid I haven't told you all. Although, as I have explained, I am no true countryman, my ideas, for what they are worth, are conceived in a rural atmosphere and an artist friend of mine, of whose work I have a high opinion, has very kindly prepared a series of sketches (head- and tail-pieces, I believe you call them) which would, I think, be a valuable addition to the book.'

'Excellent,' I said. 'Have you any of the sketches with you?'

'Yes, I have them in my case,' replied Mr. Cooper.

He drew out a large envelope and put a couple of sketches in front of me. They were clearly the work of a sensitive artist —decorative, but not mere decoration. They meant something and had a genuine relevance to the text.

'Of course,' said Mr. Cooper, 'I have paid my friend the proper fee for the drawings, but I realize that their reproduction may involve a considerable addition to the cost of printing the book.'

'It will be money well spent,' I said, 'and if it means an extra shilling on the price of the book, everyone will recognize the extra value.'

'Do you think so? I don't expect the book to be cheap. I know how small the public is for this kind of book and I know, too, how rapidly your costs have risen in recent times.'

'Forgive me, Mr. Cooper. But aren't we going ahead a little too fast? May we not first settle the terms of an agreement?'

'Well, if you are really prepared to take the book now, it would certainly be a load off my mind. I must confess that when I began, a little while ago, to visualize my work in book form, I had a hope at the back of my mind that it might appear in the dignified style which I always associate with your imprint.'

'That is very gratifying, Mr. Cooper. But, now, what about royalties?'

'Well, naturally, I should not be averse from receiving something—but only, of course, after your own heavy costs have been recovered.'

'I'm afraid the Authors' Society wouldn't approve of that. Nor, in fact, should I. What about fifteen per cent. with £50 on account?'

'I am not sure that I fully understand, but it sounds to me generous.'

'And what about American rights?'

'America? But do you think anyone in America will want the book?'

'I am sure of it. But this is the point: do you wish to reserve the American rights or would you like us to negotiate them for you?'

## THE PERFECT AUTHOR

'I would, indeed.'

'And translation rights?'

'Oh, certainly—though I cannot conceive that they can be of any value.'

'Now let me be frank about this, Mr. Cooper. If we make all arrangements for American and other special editions, we shall naturally be obliged to retain a certain fraction of the royalties we receive.'

'But of course. Naturally, I realize how heavy your overhead expenses must be in these difficult days.'

I sent for a royalty agreement form.

'Now here,' I said, 'is our standard form, Mr. Cooper. It may strike you as a long and over-elaborate document. But there are many points in copyright law about which, in your interests as well as our own, we have to be careful. We also have to make provision for various forms of sale at special prices and such prices naturally have their effect upon royalties. I don't want to burden you with these details to-day. What I suggest is that you should take this form away with you, so that you may read it carefully at your leisure. Then, when you are next in Cambridge, you can bring it back to me and we can discuss any points about which you may not feel quite happy. The last thing I wish is that you should be rushed into signing a document which you have not had time to study.'

'But, my dear sir, it is you who are rushing into what may be a most risky undertaking. It is you who have not had time to study my manuscript.' Mr. Cooper looked genuinely distressed.

'I have studied the published essays of Marmaduke Cooper with great care,' I said.

'Well, of course, if you would really like to complete this agreement to-day—and upon the generous terms you propose—I should be delighted. It would relieve me of any further anxieties on the business side and I should not have to enter into any tiresome negotiations with an agent.'

'Well, then, let us decide how we are going to fill in the blank spaces in the form. The rate of royalty and the advance we've already settled—that is, if my suggestion is really satisfactory to you?'

'Oh, certainly.'

'Now, about the title of the book, Mr. Cooper.'

'Ah, yes, I've no doubt that is important. You don't like my suggestion of "Essays in Rural Philosophy"?'

'It's perfectly good as far as it goes, Mr. Cooper, but it is not really striking. It suggests what might be a casual collection of papers. But, as I understand it, your book has a real unity.'

'Well, I like to think so. Certainly there is a single theme running through it.'

'So that "Essays in Rural Philosophy" might be perfectly suitable as a sub-title. But for the main title we ought to have something shorter, something more arresting.'

'Yes, yes. I think I see what you mean. Naturally, with your experience, you will very quickly hit upon this and other weaknesses in my presentation.'

'What about "Urbs in rure" or something of the kind? Of course, I've no right to make any positive proposal until I have read the manuscript. I merely throw out the suggestion to show the kind of thing I have in mind—from the publishing point of view.'

'Of course. Yes, I'm sure your suggestion is most valuable.'

'But we needn't worry about settling anything to-day. In the agreement we can add "or other title to be determined".'

'Certainly, certainly.'

In a few minutes my secretary brought two copies of an agreement form ready for signature. She also brought tea. Mr. Cooper was disproportionately grateful for both.

'And now,' he said, 'I really mustn't take any more of your time. I can't tell you how much obliged I am to you for all your kindness.'

'It has been a most fortunate afternoon,' I replied. 'Now, what about the manuscript? I know you still have some more work to do upon it, but will you not leave it with me for a day so that I may read it properly? I will send it back to-morrow.'

'Very well. Yes, I should like to have it back for a little while, and thank you again for—oh, and just one more question. If, when you have read the manuscript, you still feel quite sure that you would like to print it, could you give me a hint—just the roughest guess, of course—of when it might be ready for publication?'

## THE PERFECT AUTHOR

'Ah, there you touch upon one of our greatest difficulties, Mr. Cooper. We are grappling with such an accumulation of arrears at the present time that I'm afraid I couldn't hold out any hope of publishing the book in less than nine months from now. Indeed, it might well be twelve months.'

Mr. Cooper's eyebrows went up.

'Oh, but that is a great surprise to me,' he said.

'I'm sorry, Mr. Cooper. I would like to say six months, but I shouldn't be honest if I did so. You see——'

'Ah, but you misunderstand me. Of course I realize how many claims you have upon your capacity and I was fully prepared to hear that it might well be two years before my book could appear. To hear you suggest nine or twelve months was a surprise, certainly, but an agreeable surprise.'

'Well, then, we are agreed,' I said, and Mr. Cooper went.

I took the manuscript home that evening and a quiet reading of it confirmed my hopes. I foresaw no mammoth sales and I had no hope of its selection by a Book Club. But I knew that the book had quality, and quality that would endure. Faithful to my promise, I returned the manuscript to the author on the following day and about a fortnight later it came back. The corrected pages had been re-typed; the position of each drawing was clearly marked; the preliminary matter was complete with a short preface (dated and initialled) and a list of contents.

I lent the manuscript for a day to the best of our publicity people. 'Here's something that you will enjoy,' I said. 'Tear the heart out of it and let me have a really good advance notice of it—not a puff, just a statement, an under-statement if you like. It's vintage prose.'

Then I took the manuscript to the production manager, who enjoyed himself in preparing one or two 'lay-outs'. Our printer sent us two specimen pages (one in Garamond and one in Scotch Roman) and remarked that it was a pleasant change to handle some decent copy; he could let us have proofs in three weeks if we were in a hurry for them.

I sent the specimens to Mr. Cooper, expressing my personal preference for the Scotch Roman. Two days later Mr. Cooper appeared in my office.

'Yes,' he said, 'I am delighted with the appearance of the

page. I had not contemplated such a handsome type or such generous margins and I entirely agree with you in your preference for the plainer style. Both pages are most attractive, of course. In fact, I feel that they are too grand for my modest work.'

'No, no, Mr. Cooper. But now, about proofs?'

'Could I have an extra set?'

'In addition to your two sets? Certainly; more, if you like.'

'Oh, no. Two will satisfy me entirely.'

'And do you feel that you ought to have galleys?'

'Galleys? Oh yes, I know what you mean—those long slips that are so tiresome to handle. No, I certainly don't want them, unless you think I ought to have the first proof in that form.'

'Certainly not, so far as we are concerned. The illustrations are all placed in their respective chapters and we don't wish to tempt you to re-write your book when you see it in proof.'

'There need be no fear of that. It is, of course, possible that I may want to re-cast a phrase here and there, but such changes will only be slight, I can assure you. If for some unforeseen reason, I should wish to make a really extensive alteration, I should naturally expect to meet the extra expense involved.'

'The agreement entitles you to quite a substantial allowance for corrections in proof.'

'Does it, indeed? That sounds exceedingly generous. I am afraid I haven't really studied the document in detail.'

'Well, we won't worry about that now. If we are agreed on the typographical style, I can tell our printer to go ahead and I think I can promise that there will be no unreasonable delay over the proofs.'

The proofs went out at the end of a month and were returned a week later with the following letter: 'I am returning the proofs with many thanks not only for your remarkable promptitude, but for the extreme care and accuracy with which they have been prepared. Your reader's knowledge is at several points superior to mine and I have in nearly every instance accepted his emendations. I trust that the few corrections of my own will not cause undue inconvenience. The illustrations seem to me to have been beautifully reproduced and your care has been such that I shall not require a revised proof.'

## THE PERFECT AUTHOR

Meanwhile I had sent stitched proofs to a few personal friends amongst critics and booksellers, as well as to our representatives in America and elsewhere. My friends at home returned encouraging replies. The booksellers were not confident about really large sales but they had no doubts about the calibre of the work. 'It will not be the biggest seller,' wrote one of them, 'but it will certainly be the most distinguished title in the non-fiction list of the coming spring.'

A fortnight later I had a cable from our man in New York: he had had no difficulty in arranging for an American edition on good terms; and would we please send all available information (with photograph) about the author? An air-mail letter followed. Who was Marmaduke Cooper? What had he written? Where had he graduated? What were his hobbies—and his religious denomination?

I wrote at once to Mr. Cooper. I emphasized the immediacy of the appeal which the book had made in the United States, but I introduced the request for *personalia* very gently. I was not surprised at his reply: 'I am astonished, though none the less gratified, at the prospect of an American public. But why that public should desire to know the details of my private life and habits I do not understand. So far as I can recollect, I was last photographed when I had just left school.'

I compiled what facts I could about Mr. Cooper's career, added one or two discreet remarks about his position in the English world of letters and told our man in New York that he must be content with that.

The English edition went to press in due course. After a good deal of discussion with the sales manager I had decided to print five thousand copies. We had to wait some months for the paper and in writing to Mr. Cooper about presentation copies I took the opportunity of mentioning the number to him. His surprise was clearly genuine. Indeed, it amounted almost to distress:

'It is not for me,' he wrote, 'to criticize your decisions, but I can only say that I wondered, as I read your letter, whether the figure quoted in it was the outcome of a typist's error. As to presentation copies, I see that I am entitled to six under the terms of the agreement. These will amply meet my needs. I shall keep two copies for my own shelves. May I take advantage of your kind offer and ask you to dispatch the remaining four to the addresses which I enclose? You will, of course, charge the postage to me.'

We published the book on a Friday (a later Friday than I had hoped, but the binders ran out of cloth for some weeks); on the Saturday, the *Literary Supplement* described it as 'at once the most solid and the most distinguished contribution to contemporary thought'; on the Sunday there were long and laudatory notices in the two principal papers; on the Monday evening the sales department reported that the edition was exhausted.

I sat down to write to Mr. Cooper. Before I had finished, I received a letter from him. Enclosed with it was his cheque on account of royalties:

'I hasten', he wrote, 'to acknowledge the cheque which you have sent me with such thoughtful promptitude. Will you think me ungrateful if I venture to request a form of commutation? The fact is that I have long desired to present a number of standard works to a reference library in which I have for many years taken a special interest. Already I have given a few volumes from time to time, but I have not hitherto been in a position to make a really substantial gift of authoritative works of reference. Now, if I could, in effect, spend my royalty cheque in ordering sets of such works as the *Cambridge Larger Septuagint*. . . .'

The telephone bell sounded—raucously. I sat up hurriedly. The manuscript had slipped from my knees to the floor. I turned to my table and took up the receiver, barely yet awake:

'It's Mr. Robinson, sir. He says he can't understand why he hasn't had any proofs. He says it's six months since you accepted his manuscript and that if he'd known there was going to be all this delay, he'd never have——'

'Put me through,' I said wearily.